SERVANTS OR FRIENDS?

SERVANTS OR FRIENDS?

Another Look at God

GRAHAM MAXWELL

ILLUSTRATED BY
SUSAN KELLEY

Pineknoll

Publications
REDLANDS, CALIFORNIA

Text © 1992 Graham Maxwell
Illustrations © 1992 Pine Knoll Publications
All rights reserved
∞ Printed on acid-free paper in the United States of America

Published by Pine Knoll Publications · 1345 Pine Knoll, Redlands, California 92373 USA

Design: Elliot Hutkin, Susan Kelley, and Linda Wheeler
Production consultant: Elliot Hutkin
Typography: Linda Wheeler

The Library of Congress has already cataloged an earlier printing as follows:

Maxwell, A. Graham (Arthur Graham), 1921–
    Servants or friends? : another look at God /Graham Maxwell :
illustrated by Susan Kelley.
        p.   cm.
    Includes bibliographical references.
    ISBN 1-56652-000-2. — ISBN 1-56652-001-0 (pbk.)
    1. God—Biblical teaching.   2.   Friendship—Religious aspects—-
-Christianity.   I. Title.
BS544.M29   1992
231.7—dc20   92-15397
                               CIP

NRSV: Biblical citations are from the New Revised Standard Version Bible, copyright © 1989, by the Division of Christian Education of the National Council of Churches of Christ in the United States of America. Used by permission.

REB: From the Revised English Bible. Copyright © Oxford University Press and Cambridge University Press, 1989. Reprinted by permission.

GNB: Good News Bible, Today's English Version text, American Bible Society, 1976 ©. Being used by permission.

NIV: Scripture taken from the HOLY BIBLE, NEW INTERNATIONAL VERSION, Copyright © 1973, 1978, 1984 International Bible Society. Used by permission of Zondervan Bible Publishers.

KJV: King James Version

Moffatt: The Bible: A New Translation, by James Moffat. Copyright, 1954.

Phillips: The New Testament in Modern English; Hosea, from Four Prophets. Copyright © J.B. Phillips, 1958, 1960, 1972; 1963, respectively. Reprinted with permission of Macmillan Publishing Company.

Smith and Goodspeed: The Complete Bible: An American Translation. Copyright © 1923, 1927, 1948 by The University of Chicago. Used by permission of The University of Chicago Press.

NEB: From the New English Bible, copyright © by The Delegates of the Oxford University Press and The Syndics of the Cambridge University Press, 1961, 1970. Used by permission.

RSV: The Revised Standard Version of the Bible, copyrighted 1946 and 1952 by the Division of Christian Education of the National Council of Churches of Christ in the United States of America. Used by permission.

Knox: The Bible, copyright © Sheed and Ward, Inc., New York, 1950.

Cassier: God's New Covenant, The New Testament Translation, William B. Eerdmans Publishing Company. Copyright © Olive Cassirer, 1989.

Hardcover ISBN 1-56652-000-2 · Paperback ISBN 1-56652-001-0 · Book-On-Tape ISBN 1-56652-002-9

CONTENTS

PROLOGUE

ave you ever heard of a king announcing to his subjects that he will no longer treat them as his servants? Instead, if they are willing, he will take them into his confidence as trusted friends. The monarch wants it clearly understood that he has no desire for the blind, unthinking obedience of a slave. He much prefers intelligent cooperation, freely given. And to make this possible, he offers to keep his people well informed about the workings of his government.

The Bible records that Jesus made just such an incredible offer to his disciples before he returned to heaven to resume his full kingly power. John was with Jesus when he made this offer, and he recorded it in his Gospel — in the fifteenth chapter and the fifteenth verse. "I call you no longer my servants," Jesus said, "for servants simply do what they're told. I call you rather my friends, for I want you to understand."

The one the Bible describes as "King of kings and Lord of lords" prefers to regard us not as servants, but as friends. To me, this is the best of all the good news that we call the Gospel. Think of what this implies about the kind of person God must be and what it would be like to live with such a God for eternity.

During almost fifty years of college and university Bible teaching, it has been my greatest pleasure to conduct a year-long course that involves reading through each of the sixty-six books in the Old and New Testaments.[1] The purpose is to learn how to view the Bible as a whole and to see how all its parts relate to the one supreme, central subject — the truth about God himself.

As I look back over 135 such trips through all sixty-six, there is one passage that stands out ever more clearly as revealing the most important truth about God — a key to understanding the rest of Scripture and God's plan to restore peace in his universe. It is this offer of friendship recorded in John 15:15.

The purpose of *Servants or Friends?* is to consider the far-reaching and, to some believers, highly desirable implications of God's clearly stated preference for something more than just submissive service — the freedom of understanding friendship.

1 WOULD YOU BE AFRAID TO MEET GOD?

ould you be afraid to meet God?"

"Yes, terribly terrified!"

"Why so?"

The Scottish gravedigger stood in the rain among the thousands of tombstones surrounding the ancient kirk[1] where he also served as Sunday school superintendent.

"Because of all those terrifying stories in the Bible."

I had asked the same question of all kinds of people around the British Isles. It was part of a 13,000 mile trip back and forth across beautiful Britain to discover why so few in that once so Christian land still attend church regularly or profess belief in God.

I asked a saintly lady who had devoted her long life to teaching Bible to the children. "Would *you* be afraid to meet God?"

"Not at all."

"Why not?"

"Because of all those wonderful stories about God's love."

"What about all the terrifying stories in the Bible?"

"I'd be terribly terrified!"

5

"We don't concentrate on the more ferocious aspects of the Scriptures. We prefer to emphasize the loving ones."

"But what about the lake of fire in the book of Revelation?"

"Oh, with the children we don't do that last book in the Bible."

"What about the Genesis story of the flood, when God drowned all but eight?"

"Oh, the children have no difficulty with that. They have a keen sense of justice, and they especially like how God saved those eight in the ark."

The gravedigger and the Bible teacher are obviously not among those in Britain who have abandoned Christianity, as they understand it. But for many others, the "more ferocious aspects of the Scriptures," as the teacher put it, have turned them away from both God and the church.

I heard frequent references to the horrors of hell and the impossibility of trusting a god who would demand obedience under threat of eternal torment. As one Shakespearian actress somewhat heatedly complained, "The gods of other religions are less cruel than the god of the Old Testament!" She remembered only with terror the god she had known as a child, and no trustworthy god had yet taken his place.

But the people of Britain are as friendly as I have always known them to be. Home and family are still the center of society. And the warmth and friendship families may have once found in the church, many now look for somewhere else. A favorite place is the neighborhood pub.

"Why are the churches so empty and the pubs so full?"

"Better service, I expect!" was the immediate reply of a retired London ice cream vendor, as he jauntily leaned on his cane outside the boarded-up stone parish church he hoped soon to purchase and convert to a home.

"Would you be afraid to meet God?"

"Why should I? I'm not afraid of anyone. Besides, I've always been a fairly decent person, never kicked a neighbor when he's down."

"Did you attend this church before it was boarded up?"

"I haven't gone to church for years. Oh, I used to attend Sunday school when I was little. But I was pressured into going."

"Who did the pressing?"

"Mother!"

Like the retired ice cream vendor, many others spoke of their mums and grannies[2] having seen to it that they attended Sunday school. But as they grew older, unanswered questions led to disillusionment — a frequent term I heard — disillusionment with Bible, church, and God. In the land that has done so much for worldwide circulation of the Scriptures, one bookshop proprietor reported, "I'm doing well if I sell two Bibles in a year!"

Many Wish They Could Still Believe

But even as individuals and families described their unbelief, I sensed a wistful longing that there still might be Someone they could trust, a God whose actions made good sense.

"Do you sometimes wish you could still believe?"

"Yes, I do," was the unhesitating answer of an eloquent Irish commentator, who as a boy had attended no less than three churches every Sunday and could still quote Scripture from memory. "But there simply is no evidence."

On a tiny humpbacked bridge over the canal in Stratford-upon-Avon, Shakespeare's town, I talked with a muscular motorbiker who said he never had believed in God.

"Have you ever read the Bible?"

"No."

"Have you ever gone to church?"

"No."

"When we come to the end of our lives, we'll find out if there is Someone on the other side."

"That's right."

"If it turns out that there really is a God, do you expect to be afraid?"

"No. If there is a God, I'm sure he'll be 'one of the lads'" (a friendly English phrase meaning someone you would enjoy being with, someone you could trust). He didn't say this flippantly, for in earnest he added that until we know about God for sure, we ought at least to be good to each other. "There's no real 'ell," he went on. "Hell is people. People not being decent to each other."

The tough-looking but gentle motorbiker seemed as if he would welcome as good news that there really is such a God as he described. One thing for certain, though: there are widely-held pictures of God he would find impossible to entertain.

With or without earlier religious instruction, so many who professed no belief in God still spoke, vaguely to be sure, of a distant but kindly power. "A benevolent gaseous presence," was one young mother's description, with an airy wave of the hand, as she recalled childhood years of Sunday school attendance.

I met a friendly family of four walking near the beach in northwest England. The mother talked sadly about their gradual abandonment of Christian worship and belief. "God and the church are far too distant," she explained. "They don't have meaning anymore." In spite of years in church and Sunday school, no one in the family could remember a single Bible story.

"For there to be a god you could worship once again, what would he have to be like?"

Why are the churches so empty and the pubs so full? Better service, I expect"

9

Eleven-year-old Lorraine quietly answered, "He'd have to be someone I could trust, someone who'd never let me down."

Is There Someone We Can Trust?

It would do no good to try to settle this by quoting the claims of Scripture. The Bible's picture of God, as they saw it, was what had led them to doubt these claims. And recitation of the loving stories would not be enough to outweigh the "more ferocious aspects of the Scriptures." Which passages really tell the truth? To many thoughtful people the Bible has lost authority because it doesn't always seem to make good sense.

The wife of a successful businessman searched for words to describe her picture of God. "Inconsistent, arbitrary," she began, then settled finally on "cruel." "But," she continued, "why can't we keep the values of Christianity, like loving your neighbor as yourself, yet without the Christian's God?" Like so many others, she had grown up in Sunday school, but now — it seemed somewhat regretfully — declared herself "an atheist."

Not long ago Queen Elizabeth publicly observed that the people of Britain value nothing higher than their freedom and individuality. For centuries they have defended — sometimes even at risk of life — their freedom to worship in the church of their choice. Now many are exercising that same freedom by staying away.

God, the Bible, and the church are perceived not so much as a threat to this treasured freedom, but rather as simply irrelevant, belonging to a bygone age of serfs and aristocracy, when freedom was only for the privileged few, and the powerful preyed on the superstitions of the poor.

All over Britain are reminders of the years when Christianity enjoyed far greater authority. But so often they are monuments not only to individual courage and faith, but also to the long, dark history of the attempts of religion — including Christianity — to suppress freedom and individuality, often by barbarous means.

In Chester, near the northern boundary of England and Wales, is a simple stone monument beside the road that helps us to remember that more than one branch of Christianity has practiced such cruel suppression. The inscription records that George Marsh, a Protestant clergyman, was "burnt to death near this spot for the truth's sake" under Bloody Mary in 1555. It is also a monument to John Pleasington, a Roman Catholic priest, "martyred here" by Protestants in 1679, and "canonized a saint in 1970." Both heretics were put to death in the name of the same Christian God, and the crowds who enjoyed gathering to witness such proceedings could hardly be blamed for regarding God with considerable confusion and fear.

Even in recent, more enlightened times, in the minds of many people, God, the Bible, and the church are not seen as enhancing the dignity of freedom and individuality. Failing to make good sense out of Christianity, many have apparently found it easiest just to consider God and religion, along with Stonehenge and the Tower of London, as all part of Britain's colorful cultural heritage, to be preserved — even treasured, to be sure — but not as part of modern living.

Is This the End of the Christian Age?

As another motorbiker said in Stratford, "I used to believe in a friendly God, when I was a lad in Sunday school. But now I just don't need him anymore." So many seem to share this view that it has become common of late to speak of the end of the Christian age in Great Britain, as also in much of Europe.

"We don't have to go to church to be decent people,"[3] observed Barry, a gentleman butcher, as he leaned on his bright red van. When I asked him to name the imposing church just across the street from his shop, he laughed as he shook his head. "You're talking to the wrong person. I don't believe in God, and I never go to church." But Barry clearly showed the marks of a truly decent man.

When Christianity was more dominant, one might have expected that people of varying views would be correspondingly more decent and respectful to each other. But as a distinguished Oxford librarian — himself a devout Christian — has observed, "One good thing that can be said about the decline of religion in Britain is that people are now more tolerant toward each other."

It must be a great disappointment to God that so many of the decent people of Britain and all around the world identify him with a less free and less civilized time. How he must wish that they could hear the incredible offer of his Son, made almost two thousand years ago: "I call you no longer my servants. I call you rather my friends!"

What government could be more civilized, what society more free, than one presided over by the God of John 15:15?

2   I'D RATHER YOU BE MY FRIENDS

The actual words Jesus spoke to his disciples that night in the upper room[1] were in the Aramaic language. John recorded them in Greek, and here is a precise translation into English: "No longer do I call you servants…" The Greek word really means "slaves," but somehow we shrink from that harsher term. "No longer do I call you servants [or, slaves], for the servant does not know what his master [or, lord] is doing. But I have called you friends, because everything I have heard from the Father I have made known to you."

Notice the distinction Jesus drew between being a servant and being a friend. It's not the privilege of the servant to understand his master's business. It's just for him to do what he's told. No questions. No reasons. Just "Very good, sir. If you say so, sir."

To make it plain that he did not want such blind obedience, Jesus reminded the disciples that he had told them all he could about his Father's business. This would make it possible for them to give him what he really wanted — the free cooperation of understanding friends.

"Do I have to kiss my brother?"

But wouldn't it seem more appropriate for us weak, sinful mortals to settle for being unquestioning servants? In fact, a passage in Paul's letter to the Romans is used by some to support the idea that faithful servants would never presume to question God's inscrutable ways. In Romans 9:20 the apostle is responding to an evidently puzzled and somewhat indignant inquirer:

"Who are you, a human being, to argue with God? Will what has been molded say to the one who molded it, 'Why have you made me like this?'"

Such an abrupt rebuff would seem to put an end to all attempts at understanding. And admittedly this would seem entirely proper for mere human beings. "Just tell us what you want us to believe, and we'll believe it. Just tell us what you want us to do, and we'll do it." But this is servant talk and not in harmony with the offer of friendship and understanding in John 15:15. Yet how many times I have heard Romans 9:20 cited during theological discussion — which is supposed to bring the argument to a close!

It is important — more than that, essential — always to read this passage in its larger setting. In the first eight chapters of his epistle[2] to the Romans Paul has explained that God offers the freedom of friendship and salvation to all who choose to trust him. All are equally eligible, regardless of race, nationality, sex, or social standing — for God is the Father of us all.

"But that's not fair," object some in Paul's audience. "God made this offer to our father, Abraham, and only the descendants of Abraham are entitled to such high privilege."

Paul agrees. But he goes on to suggest that not all of Abraham's physical descendants have accepted God's gracious offer. The real descendants of Father Abraham are all those who, like Abraham, have chosen to be God's trusting friends.

"That's neither right nor fair!" comes the objection.

"Are you mere humans presuming to tell God how he may or may not run his universe?" is Paul's response in Romans 9:20.

God, as Creator of the universe and all of us who live in it, obviously has the sovereign right to run it any way he pleases. The good news is that he is unchangeably committed to governing it in an atmosphere of freedom and friendship, and *all* his children are invited to participate.

Romans 9:20 is not designed to discourage or prohibit reverent inquiry and friendly understanding. It is rather an expression of amazement that anyone could be so utterly impertinent — not to mention irrational — as to challenge God's right to run his universe in this wonderful way.

Of course, when you stop to think of it, how could we mere humans actually be on genuinely friendly terms with Someone who is so infinitely far above us, so awesome in power and majesty that the Bible describes mighty angels as bowing humbly in his presence?[3] How can we be close and friendly with such a powerful Being?

Or is Jesus just speaking in John 15:15 about his own very humble, approachable self, as he lived among us as a man? Could he also be including the one we call the Father? A favorite hymn is "What a Friend We Have in Jesus." But have you ever heard, "What a Friend We Have in the Father"?

Jesus had already prepared the disciples for this. "If you have seen me, you have seen the Father. If you trust me, you trust the Father." He had told them this just before he made the offer of friendship.[4] Then he added a little later, "the Father himself loves you."[5]

Besides, who is Jesus anyway? In many places in the Bible, Jesus is described as God, the Creator himself. But never is it stated more clearly than in the passage we sing every Christmas in Handel's "The Messiah."

"For unto us a child is born, unto us a son is given . . . and his name shall be called . . . The mighty God, The everlasting

Father, The Prince of Peace."⁶ We know who the Prince of Peace is. He is also mighty God, everlasting Father! This is the one who would rather call us, not his servants, but his friends.

"God Said It!" That Settles It?

But doesn't the Bible seem to say a great deal more about being obedient servants — with accompanying lists of rewards and punishments? That's true. And it's my observation that many devout saints seem to prefer the servant passages. So they try to act as they believe faithful servants should. They don't ask questions. They don't look for reasons.

They'll even say, "Faith needs no reasons." They just put on that famous bumper sticker, "God said it! I believe it! That settles it!"

Through the years there have been religious leaders who have much preferred the servant model of a believer's relationship with God. Claiming to be God's representatives, they have derived much of their own authority from this understanding and have expected their own followers to behave like loyal servants. And remember, servants don't ask, "Why?" Servants don't need reasons. Servants just obey.

Jim Jones⁷ persuaded his followers of this, and in obedience nine hundred of them drank cyanide and nine hundred of them died. If only they had asked some questions, many members of the People's Temple might still be alive. But in blind faith they submitted to the demands of their demented leader and sacrificed themselves in that 1978 mass religious suicide in the jungles of Guyana.

"Be My Friends, or I'll Destroy You"?

For those who have read the many Bible warnings of destruction, the question naturally arises: How can we be friendly with someone who threatens to burn us to death if we disobey? Is God saying, "Be my friends, or I'll destroy you"?

When Nebuchadnezzar said, "On your knees, or I'll throw you into the burning fiery furnace,"[8] he knew better than to say, "Tell me how much you love me, or I'll throw you into the fire." *You can force people to their knees, but you cannot force them to be your friends.*

"Love Me or Leave Me!"

A while ago I received a Valentine card featuring that famous cartoon cat, Garfield. The usually irascible Garfield is holding his heart in his hand and appealing so persuasively, "It's your choice…love me or leave me!" Now that's the way to win a friend, isn't it? But open up the card and inside he threatens, "Make the wrong choice and I'll break your arm!"

Be my Valentine, or I'll break your arm? That is *supposed* to sound absurd. But how, then, do you explain the fearsome warning of the third angel in Revelation 14 in the light of the appeal to friendship in John 15:15? Is God saying, "What I want most is your love and friendship, but if I don't get it, I'll torture you for eternity"? Do you find that winsome or convincing? Or is it all right to ask about the meaning? Servants don't ask questions. Friends do. Friends respectfully and reverently ask, "Why?"

"Ask at Your Own Risk!"

I have another Garfield card that pictures him holding a hammer in his upraised paw, while he ominously warns, "Ask at your own risk!" Sadly, some seem to hear God uttering the same warning. I think it's much more hazardous *not* to ask, or we might wind up drinking cyanide with Jim Jones.

The way of the Bible is to provide evidence upon which

inquiring friends can base their understanding. So you would expect the Scriptures to offer examples that demonstrate how our heavenly Father regards the serious questions of his children.

Abraham Was Called God's Friend

Think of Abraham. When God came down to destroy Sodom and Gomorrah, he first turned aside to tell his old friend what he was going to do.[9] Did Abraham respond, "Well, who am I to question your inscrutable ways? Very good, Sir. I'll be out on the hillside to watch them burn"?

No!

"God, as I know you, you couldn't do it if there were fifty decent people there, even forty, thirty, twenty, even less. Forgive me, Lord, if I seem irreverent, but should not the Judge of all the earth do what is right?"[10]

Did God reply in anger, "That's the end of our friendship. I've never heard such impertinence"?

On the contrary!

"You would have to be my understanding friend to talk to me like that. And I shall make you the model of trusting friendship throughout the rest of Scripture." And so, in both the Old and New Testaments, Abraham is mentioned as God's best friend, the one who dared to ask him, "Why?"

God Could Talk to Moses as a Man Speaks with a Friend

Later God said to Moses, "I'm sick and tired of these people. Step aside and let me destroy them. And I'll make a great nation of you."[11] Did Moses reply, "Very good, Sir. If you say so, Sir. Who am I to question your inscrutable ways? And I appreciate your offer to make me a great nation"?

He did nothing of the sort.

"God, as I know you, you wouldn't do it. Besides, if you did, it would ruin your reputation. The Egyptians would hear about it and assume you were too weak to take your people all the way to the promised land. God, as I know you, you simply couldn't!"

"Who else knows me as well as you do, Moses? You really are my friend. That's why I can talk plainly with you, face to face, as a man speaks to his friend."[12]

"Thank You, Job, for Being My Friend"

And then there was Job. In his apparent abandonment by God, he cried out, "God, you and I used to be such good friends. We talked together all the time. Why won't you talk to me now? Please tell me what's gone wrong?"[13]

Elihu and three other well-intentioned but "miserable comforters"[14] came to counsel Job. Elihu said, "I wouldn't ask to speak to God. I wouldn't give him a chance to kill me."[15] You see, Elihu at best was only a trembling servant.

But Job continued, "I *want* God to speak to me. Please speak to me, God, because I know if we could only talk together, I could come to an understanding of why all this is happening to me."[16]

In the end God intervened. "You're right, Job. Your counsellors do not know me as you do. Thank you, Job, for being my friend. Thank you for telling the truth."[17]

If only the disciples had accepted Jesus' offer of friendship, they would have felt free to ask questions right there in the upper room. Questions such as, "If you want us to be your friends, why is there so much servant talk in the Bible? Since love and friendship cannot be commanded, why is there so much use of law?"

"Tell Your Brother that You Love Him!"

Can you perhaps remember an occasion long ago when you punched your little brother in the eye? With her usual insight, Mother soon determines who's to blame.

"Tell your brother that you're sorry."

But you don't feel sorry at all. To tell the truth, you'd like to punch him in the other eye. But there's Mother standing by, and Mother's much bigger than you are. So you say, "I'm sorry." And what an empty sound it had!

Then your mother makes it worse. "Tell your brother that you love him." Do you remember how that sounded?

Then it gets even *worse.* "Kiss your dear brother."

"I can't."

"I said, 'Kiss your brother,' or you'll be in serious trouble." Can you remember the quality of that kiss?

How sad God must have been to have to gather his children at the foot of Mount Sinai[18] and order them to love him and each other, and to stop murdering and hating each other, and stop being immoral and stealing and telling lies. When a father has to do that to his children, the situation in his family must be very serious.

Love Cannot Be Commanded

As the apostle Paul explains, law was added because of wrongdoing and transgression.[19] Actually, what God wants most for his children — peace, love, happiness and trusting friendship — cannot be produced by legislation, much less by force or fear. "Not by might, nor by power, but by my Spirit," says the Lord.[20] Only by the way the Spirit works — the Spirit of love and truth — can people be persuaded of their own free will to give God what he wants.

You can force people to be your servants. But you cannot compel them to be your friends.

I wish the disciples had asked Jesus there in the upper room to explain his extensive use of law. It seems such a contradiction of experience and common sense to command people to love God and to love each other. Yet just before and just after his offer of friendship in John 15:15, he repeated the command to love. "This is my commandment: love one another, as I have loved you." "This is my commandment to you: love one another."[21]

Then Jesus added on that same occasion, "You are my friends if you do what I command you."[22] Did you ever try that on someone you wanted to be your friend?

What would have happened when you were a child in school, if you had walked up to a fellow student and said, "You can be my friend, as long as you do what I say"? If this is your idea of friendship, I'd be surprised if you have many friends.

It's an Honor to Be God's Servant

Which one of us would have dared to approach God with the incredible idea of John 15:15? "We are no longer willing to be called your servants. We insist that from now on we be addressed as friends!"

Actually, it's an honor to be God's servant. And how wonderful it would be to hear God say in the end, "Well done, you good and faithful servant." But it's God himself who offers us something better, far better — to be his understanding friends.

Nor should we make light of that bumper sticker, "God said it! I believe it! That settles it!" God has said, "I call you no longer my servants, because servants just do what they're told. I call you rather my friends, for I want you to understand." A truly good and faithful servant will live up to the meaning of that bumper sticker and take very seriously what God has said about his preference for friends.

I Would Rather Be God's Friend

Do you consider yourself God's servant or God's friend?

"Oh," you might say, "I consider myself something even better. I consider myself God's child."

Why is it better to be God's child?

"Ah, because children have rights, and I prize the rights Jesus bought for me at such price."

As I heard a man say in the pulpit the other day, "When I get to heaven and meet God, and he should wonder how a person such as I could possibly be there, all I'll have to do is show him my rights. He doesn't have to like me. All he has to do is see my right to be there."

To me, that's servant talk. And it's certainly not very friendly. Besides, I know many children who are not their father's friends. Absalom was David's son, and he was his father's worst enemy.[23]

So I would have to say for myself, I would rather be God's friend than just his child. But fortunately we can be all three. We don't have to choose.

I believe it is a great honor to be God's servant, and especially to be regarded as a faithful one.

It is also a high privilege to be called God's child.

But most of all, I'd rather be his friend. A trusting and trusted friend.

3   NO FRIENDSHIP WITHOUT TRUST

f God wants us to be his friends, why does he often seem so unfriendly in the Scriptures? Doesn't the Bible teach that if a man wants to have friends, he should himself be friendly?

It certainly seems to say that in Proverbs 18:24, especially as it has been translated in the 1611 *King James Version:*

"A man *that hath* friends must shew himself friendly: and there is a friend *that* sticketh closer than a brother."

Most people have probably discovered from their own experience the truth of the first line of this proverb. You can hardly expect to have friends if you are not friendly yourself. But to this day, Bible translators are not agreed that this was the meaning intended by the Hebrew writer. Many variations of the first line are offered in the versions.

Closer than a Brother

"May I have a word with you, Saul?"

But translators seem to be agreed on the meaning of the second line: a true friend sticks closer than a brother. The implication seems to be that the friends in the first line cannot be trusted, and many versions translate accordingly:

There are friends who pretend to be friends, but there is a friend who sticks closer than a brother. (RSV 1952)

Some friends play at friendship but a true friend sticks closer than one's nearest kin. (NRSV, 1989)

Some friendships do not last, but some friends are more loyal than brothers. (GNB, 1976)

When Jesus made the offer of friendship to his disciples, was he only "playing" at friendship? Was he only "pretending" to be so friendly? There can be no lasting friendship without mutual trust and trustworthiness. Is there good reason to trust the Son of God as "a friend who sticks closer than a brother"?

How are we to understand those "terrifying stories" that seemed so forbidding to the Scottish gravedigger, those "more ferocious aspects of the Scriptures" that the saintly Bible teacher hesitated to discuss with her young pupils? Are those passages, perhaps, to be understood as representing the character of the fearsome Father rather than his gentle Son?

Could the Father Be Like Jesus?

Philip was one of the disciples privileged to hear the Master's invitation to understanding friendship. Evidently he too had been puzzled by the apparent difference between the friendliness of Jesus and what he assumed to be the picture of the Father in the Old Testament. "Jesus," he requested, "show us the Father, and we shall be satisfied."[1]

"Have I been with you all this time, Philip, and you still don't know me?"

"But our questions are not about you," Philip persisted. "We know and love you, Lord. And even though we worship you as God's Son, we are not afraid to be so close to you here in the upper room. The one we have questions about is the Father. We want to know about the God who thundered on Sinai, who drowned the whole world in a flood,[2] who destroyed the cities of Sodom and Gomorrah;[3] the one who consumed Nadab and Abihu[4] and opened the earth to swallow up rebellious Korah, Dathan and Abiram,[5] who ordered the stoning of Achan and his family[6] and rained fire down from heaven on Mount Carmel."[7]

"Jesus, could the Father be like you?"

And the Lord replied, "If you really knew me, you would know the Father as well. Whoever has seen me has seen the Father. How can you say, 'Show us the Father'? Don't you believe that I am in union with the Father, and the Father is in union with me? If you trust me, you can trust the one who sent me."

"And as for those distressing stories of discipline and death," Jesus might have continued, "do not misunderstand them to mean that the Father is less friendly and approachable than you have found me to be. Actually it was I who led Israel through the wilderness. The command to stone Achan was mine!"

Paul understood this when he wrote, using the familiar Biblical symbol of the rock, "They all drank from the supernatural rock that accompanied their travels — and that rock was Christ."[8]

If only Philip had gone on questioning, the disciples might have heard some priceless explanations to record in the gospels. He could have asked, "Why, Jesus, did you order the stoning of Achan and his whole family but work to prevent the stoning of the woman caught in adultery? Why did you thunder so loudly on Sinai but speak so softly to us now?"

Unfortunately the disciples were more interested in who got the best places at the table and what positions they would hold in the future kingdom. So now it is *our* turn to ask questions, and Jesus invites us as his friends to pursue such understanding.

Why Did God Raise His Voice on Sinai?

Imagine being present on that awesome day when God came down on Sinai to speak to the children of Israel. The whole mountain shook at the presence of the Lord. There was thunder and lightning, fire and smoke, and the sound of a very loud trumpet.

And God said to Moses, "Keep the people back. If anyone even touches the mountain, he must be put to death. Whether animal or human being, he must be stoned or shot. Set a boundary around the mountain. If anyone breaks through to look at me, he will perish."[9]

The people were terrified. "They trembled with fear and stood a long way off. They said to Moses, 'If you speak to us, we will listen; but we are afraid that if God speaks to us, we will die.'"[10]

But Moses reassured the people that there was no need to be afraid, for Moses knew God and was his friend. Though he always approached him with deepest reverence and awe, he was not afraid. And the Lord would speak to Moses "face to face, as one speaks to a friend."[11]

Remember how fearlessly but reverently Moses responded to God's offer to abandon Israel and make a great nation of him instead.[12]

But all the way from Egypt to Sinai the people had behaved most irreverently, grumbling and complaining — in spite of the miraculous deliverance at the Red Sea and God's generous provision of water and food. How could God gain the attention of such people and hold it long enough to reveal more of the truth about himself?

Should he speak softly to the people, in a "still, small voice," as he would speak years later to Elijah at the mouth of the cave?[13] Should he sit and weep over Israel as he would centuries later, sitting on another mountain and crying over his people in Jerusalem?[14]

Only a dramatic display of his majesty and power could command the respect of that restless multitude in the wilderness. What a risk God would thereby run of being misunderstood as a fearsome deity, hardly one to be loved as a friend.

However, it was either run this risk or lose contact with his people. Without reverence for God, they would not listen or take his instruction seriously. This is why another Old Testament proverb teaches that "to be wise you must first have reverence for the Lord."[15] And God is willing to run the risk of being temporarily feared, even hated, rather than lose touch with his children.

Would You Care Enough to Do the Same?

Parents and teachers should be well able to understand this risk. Imagine yourself a grade-school teacher known for dignity and poise. In all your years of teaching you have never found it necessary to raise your voice to your young pupils. But now the principal has just urgently informed you at the door that the building is on fire and you must direct the children to leave the room as quickly as they can.

You turn and quietly announce that the building is on fire. But the room is very noisy following the excitement of recess. No one notices you standing there in front. Out of love for your roomful of children, would you be willing to shout? Still failing to gain their attention, would you care enough to climb on the

desk, even throw an eraser or two? The children might finally notice this extraordinary sight — their gentle teacher apparently angry for the first time, shouting and gesturing as they have never seen her before! They would slip stunned into their seats, perhaps frightened at what they saw.

"Now, children, please don't go home and tell your parents that I was angry with you," you might begin to explain. "I was simply trying to get your attention. You see, children, the building is on fire, and I don't want any of you to be hurt. So let's line up quickly and march out through that door."

The Risk of Discipline

Which shows greater love? To refuse to raise one's voice lest the children be made afraid? Or to run the risk of being feared and thought undignified in order to save the children in your care?

God runs this same risk every time he disciplines His people. "For the Lord disciplines those whom he loves."[16]

"Disciplines" is a better translation than the *King James Version* "chasteneth," which suggests only the idea of punishment. The original Greek word is not limited to this. It means to "educate," "train," "correct," "discipline" — all of which may call for occasional punishment, to be sure, but always for the purpose of instruction.

This explanation of the loving purpose of God's discipline is included in yet another of Solomon's proverbs:

> *My child, do not despise the Lord's discipline*
> *or be weary of his reproof,*
> *for the Lord reproves the one he loves,*
> *as a father the son in whom he delights.*[17]

Shall I throw an eraser or two?

The book of Hebrews cites this proverb and then urges God's children not to overlook the encouraging meaning. "God is treating you as sons. Can anyone be a son and not be disciplined by his father? If you escape the discipline in which all sons share, you must be illegitimate and not true sons. Again, we paid due respect to our human fathers who disciplined us; should we not submit even more readily to our spiritual Father, and so attain life? They disciplined us for a short time as they thought best; but he does so for our true welfare, so that we may share his holiness. Discipline, to be sure, is never pleasant; at the time it seems painful, but afterwards those who have been trained by it reap the harvest of a peaceful and upright life."[18]

A Lesson Learned on the Bottom Stair

I realize now how much my gentle mother ran this risk of being misunderstood every time she determined there was need for some especially impressive instruction. The usual place for the administration of this discipline was in the front entrance hall of our two-story home in England. On one wall stood a tall piece of furniture with a mirror, places for hats and umbrellas, and a drawer in the middle for gloves. In the drawer were two leather straps. I never discovered why there were two, but in imagination I can still hear the rattling of the handle on that drawer and the ominous shuffling of the straps as Mother made her selection. Then we would proceed together toward the stairs.

After Mother was seated and the culprit had assumed the appropriate posture, it was her custom to discuss the nature and seriousness of the misdemeanor committed, all to the rhythmical swinging of the strap. The more serious the crime, the longer it took Mother to discuss it! I cannot recall ever having thought while in that painful position, "How kind and loving of my mother to discipline me like this! How gracious she is to run the

Waiting for repentence to come.

35

risk of being misunderstood or perhaps of causing me to hate her and obey her out of fear!" On the contrary, I seem to recall very different feelings at the time.

But when it was all over, I had to sit on the bottom stair and reflect on the experience for a while. And before I could run out and play again, I always had to find Mother and there would be hugging and kissing and reassurance that things would be better from now on.

Sometimes repentance was a little slow in coming. I can remember climbing to a higher stair so that I could look out through the stained-glass windows at the flowers around the lawn. But it was hard to stay angry for long or to go on feeling afraid. Mother never seemed to lose her temper. We knew there was nothing she'd be unwilling to do for us children, and no limit to her patience in listening to all we had to tell. She seemed so proud of our successes and so understanding when we failed.

Recently I visited that bottom stair again. The stained-glass windows were still there, but the stair seemed a bit lower when I sat on it this time. Somehow I couldn't remember the pain and embarrassment of it all. But as I thought about my mother, who's been gone for many years, I did feel a specially warm sensation — but not where I used to feel it during the swinging of that strap!

I hope I shall never lose the meaning of those sessions with Mother at the bottom stair. She helped us learn an essential truth about God. Not that we understood it right away. Mother was willing to wait. And if we had grown up fearing and hating her for those times of discipline and punishment, it would have broken her heart. But she cared enough about us to be willing to run that risk.

God Much Prefers the Still, Small Voice

The message of Scripture is that God cares enough about his people to run this same risk. It is true that if we insist on having our own way, God will eventually let us go. He does not give us up easily, however. He persuades; he warns; he disciplines. He would much rather speak to us quietly as he finally could with Elijah. But if we cannot hear the still, small voice, he will speak through earthquake, wind, and fire.[19]

Sometimes, at very critical moments, it has been necessary for God to use extreme measures to gain our attention and respect. On such occasions our reluctant reverence has been largely the result of fear. But God has thereby gained another opportunity to speak, to warn us again before we are hopelessly out of reach, to win some of us back to trust — and to find that there really is no need to be afraid.

Surely in all this God has shown himself to be a friend who "sticks closer than one's nearest kin."[20] The one who wants us to be his friends is so good a friend himself that he is willing to stick with us when we are not very friendly toward him. Patiently he works to change even his enemies into understanding friends.

How God Won Saul

God "stuck" with his enemy Saul and turned him into Paul, the great apostle of trust and love. Before Saul met Jesus on the Damascus road, he was utterly dedicated to eradicating what he believed to be dangerously false teachings about God. If anyone had dared suggest that he was actually God's enemy, Saul would have been highly incensed. He had reason to regard himself as God's most zealous, hardworking servant and defender of the truth.

But Saul worshipped an unfriendly god who would use force to have his way. So in the name of the god he knew, Saul tried to force the early Christians to give up their heresy and come back to the truth. If they refused, he would have them arrested and even destroyed — just as he believed his god would do.

That's why Saul could assist in stoning so good a man as Stephen. He did not enjoy the execution, but he "approved of their killing him."[21] He remembered the story of Sinai. Did not the just and holy God direct that the disobedient should be stoned or shot?

"Please Forgive Saul"

How could God win a man like Saul to be his friend, the friend of a friendly God?

The Lord chose to confront his future friend on the road to Damascus. Saul was troubled by his memories of that execution. Stephen had shown remarkable knowledge of the Scriptures, and Saul's conscience still acknowledged the authority of truth.

Perhaps especially disturbing was Stephen's prayer of forgiveness just before he died: "Lord, do not hold this sin against them."[22] There were reports that the heretic Jesus had behaved the same way on the cross: "Father, forgive them; they do not know what they are doing."[23] If these two men really were ungodly heretics, how could they endure such torture with such godlike grace?

But, Saul could have reasoned, what about all those stories of divine wrath and retribution, the exercise of justice in stamping out sinners and sin? Had not the chief administrators and theologians authorized him to carry out this unpleasant but holy mission? So Saul continued on his way to Damascus, "still breathing threats and murder against the disciples of the Lord."[24]

Would it have done any good for God to tap him gently on the shoulder and inquire, "One moment, Saul, could I have a word with you?" Saul wouldn't even have felt God's touch. He certainly couldn't have heard the still, small voice. First something dramatic must be done to capture Saul's attention.

In a blaze of light, God floored him right there on the road. More than that, to ensure his undivided attention to what God had to say, he took away his eyesight for a while.

As Saul lay helpless on the road, he must have been shocked to discover that his assailant was none other than the meek and gentle Heretic he had once despised as weak — teaching such nonsense as loving our enemies and even praying for the Romans!

"But he could have killed me just now," Saul may have thought to himself. "I would have, if I'd been in his place. Why is he not destroying me the way I've been destroying his disciples? Instead, I hear him talking to me softly in my own language.[25] And he's talking about my conscience!

"I'm sorry, Lord. I was terribly wrong. Now please accept me as your servant, and tell what you want me to do." Years later, in his letter to the believers in Rome, Saul — now called Paul — was honored to introduce himself as "a servant, or slave, of Jesus Christ."[26]

Paul, the Servant

But God wanted more from Saul than just submissive service. So he gave him no specific orders at that time, except to get up and go on to Damascus. "There you will be told all that you are appointed to do."[27]

A man named Ananias met him in the city with the friendly welcome, "Saul, my brother, receive your sight again!"[28] Then Ananias went on to give a description of God's great expectations of his new disciple. Saul was to be God's assistant [29] in making known the truth. "The God of our fathers," Ananias continued, "appointed you to know his will and to see the Righteous One and to hear him speak, because you are to be his witness to tell the world what you have seen and heard." [30]

Paul, the Understanding Friend

As Paul reflected on God's persuasive skill in treating him so firmly but graciously on the Damascus road, he was changed into more than a faithful servant. He became a most understanding friend, whose highest aim was to witness to the truth about his Lord by treating others as God had treated him.

"Imitate me, as I imitate Christ," he wrote to the Corinthians. [31] Never again would he resort to the abuse of force. To those who disagreed with him — even about important matters — he would say, "Let everyone be fully convinced in his own mind." [32] And of those who felt free to criticize and condemn, he would ask, "Who are you to pass judgment on another?" [33]

Paul showed how well he knew God, and understood the ways of friendship and trust, by his Christ-like dealing with grossly misbehaving members of the church in Corinth. At first he appealed to them with reason and love. It was to them that he wrote the famous chapter on love that we now know as 1 Corinthians 13. But they were not impressed, and disdainfully rejected his advice.

Before Damascus, Paul would have known exactly what to do — imprison them, have a few of them stoned! But now, of course, this was out of the question. He decided to visit them in person, travelling from Ephesus to Corinth. There he was rudely insulted as weak and vacillating. They scorned his claim to be an apostle and challenged his authority to correct them at all.

Some scoffed, "His letters are weighty and strong, but his

bodily presence is weak, and his speech contemptible."[34] Obviously they would not take him seriously until he did something to win their respect.

Paul returned to Ephesus to decide his next move. It seemed clear that more gentle talk about love would only worsen the problem. Like the teacher in the burning school, should he risk misunderstanding by sternly raising his voice? Would they then accuse him of more vacillation, of contradicting his own chapter on love?

He was committed to following the example of Christ — if only he could know what the Lord would do in such a situation. But he *did* know. Christ raised his voice on Sinai to win respect and attention. He raised it again on the Damascus road, for which his former foe will be eternally grateful.

Paul made his decision. He sent a blistering letter. It was so stern that he cried as he wrote it. Worried that he might be misunderstood, he couldn't wait for a reply, and started out again for Corinth. He began to regret what he had written, but only for a while. For on the way he received the news that the emergency measure had succeeded. Raising his voice had worked! The letter had been received with "fear and trembling." And with new-found respect, the apostle's advice had been fully accepted.[35]

Can the God Who Stoned Achan Be Trusted?

As Paul cried while writing to the sinners in Corinth, so God, too, must have wept as he ordered the execution of Achan and his whole family. And he required their fellow Israelites to stone them, then burn the remains. Could such a God ever be trusted as a friend?

As they crossed the border into hostile Canaan, the people's only hope of survival lay in taking God seriously enough to

41

follow his instructions in every detail. There was danger that Achan's rebellious and disrespectful spirit would spread throughout the camp.[36]

In a day when life was held all too cheaply — the people had already told Joshua that anyone who disobeyed him should be put to death — it was necessary that God's discipline be sufficiently awful and dramatic to make an adequate impression.[37] But as the stones were finding their target, how the one who even sees the little sparrow fall[38] must have hated every horrible moment!

A Consistent Picture of God

A hundred and thirty-five trips through all sixty-six books, in company with thousands of people, have served to convince me that the Biblical record reveals a consistent picture of an infinitely powerful but equally gracious and trustworthy God, whose ultimate purpose for his children is the freedom of understanding friendship.

As he works toward this goal, he is willing to stoop and meet us where we are, leading us no faster than we're able to follow, speaking a language we can respect and understand. To keep open the channels of communication, he has often resorted to measures that risk misunderstanding.

To his enemies and careless observers, these are acts of an unfriendly God. But to understanding friends, they are further evidence of God's trustworthiness that is the basis of their trust.

And without such trust, there can be no true friendship.

4   TRUST CANNOT BE COMMANDED

n your knees, or I'll throw you in the fire!"

Nebuchadnezzar, king of Babylon and ruler of the great Babylonian empire, was now demanding that the people worship *him*. He had just erected an enormous gold image—ninety feet high and nine feet wide—and had summoned all the officials of his kingdom to attend the dedication. The whole story is recorded in the Old Testament book of Daniel.[1]

When all were assembled, a herald announced the king's command that when the musical signal was given, everyone was to bow before the image that had been set up. Anyone who refused was to be "thrown forthwith into a blazing furnace."[2]

Nebuchadnezzar saw nothing inappropriate in commanding worship under threat of such fiery destruction. Did not the gods themselves threaten similar retribution on those who incurred their displeasure?

Twenty-five centuries later, many of us find the king's call to worship incredibly cruel and uncivilized. But was he any more cruel than the apostle Paul—before his experience on the Damascus road—when, "breathing out threats and murder," he

"On your knees, or I'll throw you in the fire!"

tried to force people to submit to his fearsome god? And are there not millions in this modern age who believe in a god who demands not only their submission, but even their love and trust — all under threat, not just of death in a blazing furnace, but of eternal torture in the flames?

The music sounded, and everyone knelt — except three young Jews, Shadrach, Meshach, and Abed-nego. They had been brought to Babylon as captives during the conquest of Judah. But Nebuchadnezzar had chosen them for education in the affairs of the royal court, and recently had elevated them to positions of leadership in his empire. The king was furious to learn of their disobedience, and summoned them into his presence.

"Is it true, Shadrach, Meshach, and Abed-nego, that you do not serve my gods or worship the gold image which I have set up? Now if you are ready to prostrate yourselves...and to worship the image that I have made, well and good. But if you do not worship it, you will be thrown forthwith into the blazing furnace; and what god is there that can deliver you from my power?"[3]

The young men respectfully refused, and explained that the God whom they served was well able to look after them. Livid with rage, Nebuchadnezzar ordered that the fire be heated to seven times its usual heat and that the three be bound and thrown into the furnace.

How God Disciplined Nebuchadnezzar

How could God correct a man of such arrogance and power? How could he even communicate with a tyrant so accustomed to having his own way that he would destroy any who opposed?

Of course, God could easily have consumed him as he sat there on his throne. Onlookers would have been impressed. But destruction does not discipline the one destroyed. And the heavenly Father was only just beginning the instruction of his brilliant but arrogant child.

One thing Nebuchadnezzar respected was superior power. When Daniel had been able to remind the king of a dream he had forgotten, Nebuchadnezzar had prostrated himself at the prophet's feet. " 'Truly,' he said, 'your God is indeed God of gods and Lord over kings, and a revealer of secrets, since you have been able to reveal this secret.'"[4]

God meets people where they are. So, as he met Moses at the burning bush,[5] God met Nebuchadnezzar in the flames of the fiery furnace.

"Then King Nebuchadnezzar, greatly agitated, sprang to his feet, saying to his courtiers, 'Was it not three men whom we threw bound into the fire?' They answered, 'Yes, certainly, your majesty.' 'Yet,' he insisted, 'I can see four men walking about in the fire, free and unharmed; and the fourth looks like a god.'"[6]

The king called to the young men to come out of the furnace. Then he publicly announced:

Blessed be the God of Shadrach, Meshach, and Abed-nego! He has sent his angel to save his servants who, trusting in him, disobeyed the royal command; they were willing to submit themselves to the fire rather than to serve or worship any god other than their own God.[7]

God had clearly won the king's attention and respect. But Nebuchadnezzar still didn't know God very well — not nearly as well as did Paul after the Damascus road experience. The king was still far from being able to say with Paul, "If anyone should disagree with me, he is free to make up his own mind."[8]

Instead, Nebuchadnezzar issued another tyrannical decree:

Anyone, whatever his people, nation, or language, if he speaks blasphemy against the God of Shadrach, Meshach, or Abed-nego, is to be hacked limb from limb and his house is to be reduced to rubble; for there is no other god who can save in such a manner.[9]

By a show of power, God had led Nebuchadnezzar to take the first step toward reverence and a willingness to listen. The king, in his turn, resorted to the use of power to intimidate his people into showing due respect for this powerful god.

Nebuchadnezzar was obviously not ready yet for the gracious offer of friendship in John 15:15.

On one recorded occasion, Daniel did venture to inform the king that God was expecting him to treat his subjects with greater kindness: "Therefore, O king, be pleased to accept my advice: Renounce your sins by doing what is right, and your wickedness by being kind to the oppressed."[10] And earlier, Nebuchadnezzar had expressed admiration for the trust in God shown by the three young Hebrew exiles.

Finally, after several years of humbling discipline, the king was persuaded to publicly acknowledge that "the Most High is sovereign over the realm of humanity and gives it to whom he will."

*He does as he pleases with the host of heaven
and with those who dwell on earth.
No one can oppose his power
or question what he does.*[11]

"Now I, Nebuchadnezzar, praise and exalt and glorify the King of heaven; for all his acts are right and his ways are just, and he can bring low those whose conduct is arrogant."

"It is my pleasure," the king declared, "to recount the signs and wonders which the Most High God has worked for me: How great are his signs, how mighty his wonders!"[12]

Nebuchadnezzar was still especially impressed with power, though he did also recognize that God's use of power was right and just. But this time he did not follow his confession with a harsh decree that any who refused to join him in submission to the God of heaven should be "hacked limb from limb" or thrown into the blazing fire.

I wonder if Nebuchadnezzar ever went on to become more than a humble servant who acknowledged his Master's sovereign authority. The Bible story of his life ends without any mention of his teaching the people about love and trust — so different from the record of God's friends Moses and Paul. Perhaps Nebuchadnezzar will have to learn about the freedoms of friendship in the life to come. As a reverent and teachable servant, he would be willing to listen.

"Not by Might nor by Power"

The place where Nebuchadnezzar ordered the people to their knees is not far from the modern city of Baghdad, the capital of Iraq. It has been reported that the ruler of that country greatly admires the king of ancient Babylon. But his admiration has not led to a time of peace among the nations of the Middle East. If only Nebuchadnezzar could have served as a model of leadership among friends, of government committed to unity that is based on trust and not on force and fear. But then, of course, if the king of Babylon had been that kind of leader, some modern empire builders would not have considered him so worthy of their admiration!

How God must wish that trust and friendship could be restored in that part of the world where so many of the people are the children of his old friend Abraham. Then why doesn't the omnipotent One step in and impose his sovereign will? Didn't Jesus himself teach that "with God all things are possible"?[13] Would anyone dare suggest that there is anything God cannot do? But if by the exercise of might and power he could turn everyone in the Middle East—not to mention the rest of the world—into loving, trusting friends, then who is to blame for continuing suspicion and hostility?

God answered these questions himself. And the rest of the Bible is a demonstration of the truthfulness and significance of his explanation. " 'Not by might nor by power, but by my Spirit,' says the Lord Almighty."[14]

This message was passed on by the prophet Zechariah to Zerubbabel, the leader of the Israelites who had recently returned to Judah from Babylonian exile. After 70 years of discipline in captivity, the people were being offered yet another chance to show themselves worthy descendants of their father Abraham, a chance to live together in such peace and harmony that Jerusalem would become known as "the City of Truth," the "City of Faithfulness."[15]

It could be such a safe and friendly place that "once again men and women of ripe old age will sit in the streets of Jerusalem, each with cane in hand because of his age. The city streets will be filled with boys and girls playing there."[16]

Reports of the honesty and kindness of the inhabitants of Jerusalem would spread so far that "many peoples and powerful

nations will come to Jerusalem to seek the Lord Almighty...
In those days ten men from all languages and nations will take
firm hold of one Jew by the hem of his robe and say, 'Let us go
with you, because we have heard that God is with you.'"[17]

This is what God had always wanted for the descendants
of his old friend Abraham—and not only for them, but for all
who through the friendship and trustworthiness of Abraham's
children would come to know the truth about Abraham's God.

But God's message to Zerubbabel was that, much as he
longed to help Israel become such people, it could not be accomplished by might and power, but only by the way the Spirit
works. And while no one can oppose God's *power*, as Nebuchadnezzar finally conceded, it is still possible for the weakest human
to say no to the still small voice of love and truth.

By might and power God called into existence the whole
vast universe. But even infinite power could not hold the loyalty
of Lucifer,[18] his most brilliant angel, or convince many of the
children of Adam and Eve to love and trust their Creator.

By might and power—when he had almost lost contact
with the human race—God sadly drowned the whole world in
a flood. But might and power could not win the trust of the
descendants of Noah. They had no doubts about the existence
of God. They acknowledged his superior power. But like the
devils described in the book of James, their thoughts about God
made them tremble with fear.[19] It could be said that they believed in God, but they had no desire to trust him as a friend.
Instead, they built the tower of Babel to escape him.

By might and power God rescued his people from Egyptian bondage and established them in the land of Canaan. But all
his power could not win their trust. Again and again they
showed more faith in the cruel gods of paganism. King Solomon

once knew God so very well that with inspired wisdom he could author the book of Proverbs. But later even he sacrificed some of his own children to the fiery god Molech.[20]

"'But by My Spirit,' says the Lord Almighty"

It was not lack of might and power that led God to send the message to Zerubbabel. It was "the Lord Almighty" who was speaking. Who would know better the limitations of the use of power? Some understand Zechariah 4:6 to emphasize that the purposes of God can not be accomplished by *human* might or *human* power, but only by the might and power of God himself. But the contrast in this passage is between the use of power and the way the Holy Spirit works.

The things that God desires the most — lasting peace, freedom, trust, and friendship — can not be produced by force, much less by fear. If all God wanted was submission and unthinking service, he could readily have it in a moment. "On your knees, or I'll throw you into the fire!" But God is no heavenly Nebuchadnezzar. He would rather die than govern by force and fear. And someday, to make this eternally clear, it would indeed cost him his death.

Jesus explained how the Spirit works. He teaches, he persuades, he pleads. It's not that the Spirit possesses less might and power than the Father and the Son, for he too is God. But he works especially with the greatest and most enduring power of all — the persuasive authority of truth. Paul speaks of the power of truth to win people back to trust.[21]

But this kind of power is not recognized by everyone. It is only effective with those who are willing to listen, those who are the most deeply stirred, not by the thunders of Sinai, but by the truth spoken softly in love.

The Spirit pleaded softly with Judas while the Master

washed his betrayer's dirty feet. The loyal angels must have been overwhelmed to watch the Creator of the universe, the one they worshipped and adored, willingly on his knees in humble service to his disloyal disciple. The Holy Spirit was speaking to the angels too, and their understanding of the graciousness of God must have been greatly enlarged that evening in the upper room.

But Judas, the betrayer, remained unmoved. He said no to the gentle voice of the Holy Spirit. Why didn't an indignant God destroy him for so ungratefully refusing such loving persuasion? The angels were still learning as the Father sadly left yet another of his disloyal children to reap natural consequence. A few hours later, in the darkness of his rejection of the truth, Judas committed suicide.

Years later, the Spirit inspired John to write a description of that memorable event, so that we in our time could read it. Then, perhaps, some of us would be powerfully stirred, as were the angels, to greater trust in so gracious a God.[22]

Such trust is not commanded. It is not produced by threat of destruction. It is won by the truth about God, so movingly portrayed there in the upper room, and on hundreds of other occasions recorded in the sixty-six books.

This is the powerful way the Holy Spirit seeks to accomplish God's purpose to fill his universe with trusting and trusted friends. " 'Not by might nor by power, but by my Spirit,' says the Lord Almighty."

5   BE CAREFUL WHAT YOU TRUST

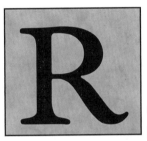

Recent polls have reported that the most trusted people in our society are ministers and physicians. The least trusted are politicians and used-car salesmen—though some think attorneys should be at the bottom. I once saw a T-shirt displaying a hungry shark with the accompanying message, "Sharks don't eat lawyers: professional courtesy!"

All of this may be quite unfair to these professions. It is certainly unfair to representatives of these professions who actually are models of trustworthiness. And the fact that a person has chosen to be a minister of the Gospel does not guarantee that he is perfectly trustworthy. All too frequently, tragedies in the news are evidence to the contrary.

Polls have also been conducted to measure recent trends in people's opinions about the trustworthiness of God. It appears that even in many parts of the so-called Christian world, trust in God has been seriously eroded.

"Watch out, and do not let anyone fool you."

God must be sad to see these trends. But not for the more obvious reason, that people seem to be trusting him less. Are people rejecting the friendly God of Abraham, Moses and Job, the God who is just like Jesus, the God who wants us to be his friends?

It could even be a cause for hope that thoughtful people are finding it impossible to trust a god who is indeed not worthy of their trust. What must bring great sorrow to God is that so many of his children don't really know what he's like.

During trips around Britain I often asked people who professed little or no faith in God, if there had ever been a time in their lives when they *did* believe.

"Oh, yes," was a not infrequent reply. "I used to believe when I was little."

"Tell me what you thought God was like back then."

When they had finished their description, often I would have to agree that if God really was like that, I wouldn't trust him myself.

Our first goal was to learn of *their* views, but — when it seemed appropriate — I would venture to suggest that there was, perhaps, another way of looking at God. "Is it possible," I would sometimes ask, "that God has been misrepresented or misunderstood?"

Sometimes, the kindness of that English, Irish, Welsh or Scottish face, would lead me to presume to add, "What would you think if God should actually be an infinitely powerful but equally gracious Person who values nothing higher than our freedom and individuality, a God who prefers to treat us not as servants but as friends?"

"I wish I could believe that," was one wistful answer.

"If I could be sure that was the truth, I suppose I'd become a believer," was the essence of other replies.

Does It Make Sense to "Believe by Faith"?

How can God convince his children of the truth about himself?

"That's something one accepts by faith," is the traditional response of many a devout believer.

"By faith in what?" you might inquire.

No, I don't mean by faith in something or somebody," the believer replies. "I mean there are some things you can only know by faith itself."

This is using the word "faith" to describe a way of knowing something in the absence of sufficient evidence, or any evidence at all. There's even a legend that a schoolboy once defined faith as "believin' wotcha know ain't so." Surely few believers would go that far. But some have explained that "faith is believing when common sense says you shouldn't." Could this be why many find it hard to believe in God? Is it because they are simply unable or unwilling to do something that goes against their common sense?

All their lives children hear their parents and teachers urge them to please use more common sense. Should we tell them that when it comes to the question of trusting God, they should feel safe to abandon this guide?

"I Just Know that It's True!"

After high school, I had the privilege of attending a small Christian college. There I met the girl who has been my wife and friend for nearly 50 years. As was the custom at such institutions, the men's and women's dormitories were prudently located at opposite ends of the campus. By today's standards, the rules for social behavior would be considered impossibly old-fashioned and strict.

In the beguiling warmth of spring each year, when a certain peach tree in the center of the campus began to bloom, friendships would blossom around the school, and the faculty would redouble their efforts to protect the academic interests of the students in their care.

When it appeared that a young man was in danger of making a premature or ill-advised commitment, the much-revered dean of women would invite him into her office for some earnest consultation.

"Young man," she would begin with kind solemnity, "you really have not had much opportunity to become well acquainted with this young woman." (Under the regulations, this was unavoidably the truth!)

"Don't you think common sense suggests that you should come to know her much better before making a final decision? Perhaps you could visit her at home next summer, see how she treats her parents and offers to help around the house." (As I said, things were quite old-fashioned in those days!)

"I don't need to know her any better," the student might politely demur. "I've even prayed about the matter, and I have a warm feeling of conviction that she's the one God wants me to choose as my wife."

"We know, young man, do we not, that it isn't safe just to trust one's feelings — especially at this time of the year. You can never be too careful in choosing the person with whom you will spend the rest of your life."

"But didn't you tell us, dean, in chapel the other day, that when it comes to deciding about giving our hearts to God, we should not be so doubting and ask so many questions, the way we do in science or history? Are you telling me that when it comes to choosing a life companion, we cannot investigate too thoroughly? But when it comes to choosing the God with whom we shall spend eternity, we can safely trust our hearts instead of our heads?"

"Young man, that's the difference between secular knowledge and religious faith. When it comes to spiritual things, we must never let our heads get in the way of our hearts."

"Thank you, dean, for your advice. But I've already made up my mind. In fact, she's already accepted my proposal and you're invited to the wedding. But don't worry, it's going to be all right. I just know in my heart that she's the one for me."

I recently heard a preacher loudly affirm, "I believe God can be trusted because by faith I know it's true. Do you want to know how I can be so sure of the truth? I just know that I know that I know that it's true!" (Actually he went on for several more "I knows!")

"Where does such faith come from?" you might further inquire.

"It's a gift of God, a fruit of the Holy Spirit."

"Then why doesn't everyone have this gift?"

"Oh, God only gives faith to the ones he chooses. And if this should tempt you to think of God as arbitrary and unfair, remember Paul's warning in Romans 9:20 about not questioning God's inscrutable ways."

But many *have* dared to question this apparent arbitrariness and, failing to find a better explanation, have been turned away from trusting such a God.

Can One Reject the Gift of Faith?

There is another way of explaining why everyone does not possess the gift of faith. It has been argued that for God to give faith to some and not to everyone violates two other precious gifts of God—freedom and the power of choice. They believe that God indeed offers his gift of faith to everyone, and everyone has the freedom and power to accept or reject. Unfortunately, some choose to refuse.

Many who take this position, however, still understand

faith to mean a God-given ability and willingness to believe without supporting evidence. That still leaves the question: On what basis does one make the vital decision to accept or reject the gift of faith? Is the acceptance of God's gift of faith an act of faith itself—a faith which is not yet received? Does this appeal to your common sense? Recalling that earlier description of faith, I find it impossible to believe when common sense says I shouldn't.

What Is the Difference Between Belief, Faith, and Trust?

Frequently the attempt is made to draw important distinctions between faith, belief and trust. In reading what the New Testament has to say about these subjects, one needs to be aware that the three English synonyms, *faith*, *belief* and *trust*, are all translations of the same Greek word *pistis*. Since many English versions of the Bible use these words interchangeably, one must beware of making distinctions between the meanings of these terms as if there were three different words in the Greek.

For example, when the jailer in Philippi asked Paul and Silas what he had to do to be saved, they gave a reply that has been the subject of many serious sermons. But what exactly did they say? [1]

"Believe on the Lord Jesus," are the familiar words of the 1611 *King James Version*.

"Put your faith in the Lord Jesus," says the 1989 *God's New Covenant* translation.

"Put your trust in the Lord Jesus," reads the 1989 *Revised English Bible*.

Belief, faith, trust—they're all essentially the same. Whether the faith and trust are genuine, and the belief more than just opinion or hope, must be determined from the context. The book of James observes that even the devils can be said to have *faith* in God. Or, when speaking about God's enemies, should it be translated *belief*? The Greek word is the same. In the context, James explains what it is about God that they *trust*, and it makes them shudder with fear.[2]

Is Trust in God a Leap in the Dark?

God wants our trust, or we can never have the friendship of John 15:15. But he does not ask us to trust him as a stranger. To trust someone we do not know could indeed be a hazardous gamble, a dangerous leap in the dark. God would not encourage running such risk.

Think of the lengths to which he has gone to make himself well known. "In many and various ways, he has spoken to us by the prophets." More than that, he has "spoken to us by his Son" — the one who could say at the end of his matchless life, "If you have seen me, you have seen the Father."[3]

The way Jesus lived, the way he treated people, the things he taught about his Father, and most of all the unique and awful way he died, were the clearest revelation of the truth about the trustworthiness of God the universe will ever see or need.

This assumes, of course, that one has confidence in the Biblical record. To trust the Bible does not require an uninformed leap in the dark. There are other religious documents that invite this "leap of faith." But the Bible itself urges a careful look at the evidence before making the decision to trust.

An Old Accusation

According to the story in the book of Genesis, the first to argue that God should not be trusted was the serpent in the garden of Eden. The book of Revelation, the last of the sixty-six, identifies the accusing serpent as "the Devil and Satan, the deceiver of the whole world." He is described as the leader of the rebellion in heaven that resulted in his being "thrown down to this earth, and his angels were thrown down with him."[4] The names *Devil* and *Satan* both mean *slanderer, adversary.* Even Jesus, who was so gracious with the worst of sinners, called him "a liar and the father of lies."[5]

"God has lied to you," Satan insinuated to the first parents of the human race. "How can you trust a god who doesn't tell the truth? If you eat of the forbidden tree[6] you will not die. Actually, eating the fruit of that tree will make you more like God. How could he selfishly deprive you of something so beneficial? And how could he be so heartless and unforgiving as to threaten you with death on just the first offense? A loving god would at least give a second chance. 'Obey me, or you'll die!' How can you worship someone so vengeful and severe? Such a demanding and arbitrary god is not worthy of your worship and trust."

If God really is the kind of person Satan has made him out to be, the Adversary is right that it would make no sense to trust such a tyrant. And there certainly could be no possibility of establishing the freedom and friendship offered by Jesus to his disciples.

But the one against whom Satan levelled his charges was friendly Jesus himself. For the one who came to bring us the truth is the Creator of the universe.[7]

God's Reply

Has God responded to these accusations? Do we find his answers a sufficient basis for our trust?

Mere denials are not enough to meet such charges. Even if the denials come from God himself, how would we know if his claims are true? Satan has also made his claims, sometimes with great show of authority and force.

But neither claims nor display of superior power can establish integrity and trustworthiness. Jesus himself warned against believing mere claims, even when apparently supported by super-natural power.

He spoke of religious leaders who would arise, making all kinds of false claims — even claiming to be Christ! They would perform great miracles and wonders to prove the truthfulness of their claims. "But don't believe them," Jesus said.[8]

"Watch out," he warned, "and do not let anyone fool you. Many men, claiming to speak for me, will come and say, 'I am the Messiah!' and they will fool many people."[9]

"My dear friends," the apostle John later advised, "do not believe all who claim to have the Spirit, but test them to find out if the spirit they have comes from God. For many false prophets have gone out everywhere."[10]

In his description of Satan's effort to sweep the whole world into his camp just before the second coming of Christ, John speaks of the Devil's use of authority and power accompanied by the performance of great miracles, even making "fire come down out of heaven to earth in the sight of everyone." As a result, "all the people living on earth" are deceived "by means of the miracles" — except God's loyal few.[11]

Prophets, Too, Can Lie

Long ago Moses had warned the children of Israel not to be misled by the working of miracles. "A prophet or an interpreter of dreams may promise a miracle or a wonder, in order to lead you to worship and serve gods that you have not worshiped before. Even if what he promises comes true, do not pay any attention to him."[12]

In the Old Testament, the story is told of a prophet from Judah who was sent by God to deliver a message to King Jeroboam. Upon completion of his mission, he was to refuse any offer of hospitality and return home by another way.

This "man of God" was a faithful servant of the Lord and accustomed to obeying without question the voice of authority. "God said it! I believe it! That settles it!" was his humble but vulnerable way of determining truth.

The prophet delivered his message. And when the king invited him to stay and eat, there was no hesitation in the reply. "'Even if you gave me half of your wealth, I would not go with you or eat or drink anything with you. The Lord has commanded me not to eat or drink a thing, and not to return home the same way I came.'"[13]

The sons of an old prophet, who lived nearby, told their father about the messenger from Judah and what he had said to the king.

"Which way did he go?" the old man asked.

They showed him the road. "Saddle my donkey," he ordered his sons, then set out to follow the obedient younger man. He found him sitting under an oak tree on the way.

"Are you the prophet from Judah?" the old man asked.

"I am."

"Then come home and have a meal with me."

"I can't. God has strictly forbidden me to stop and eat with anyone on this trip. And when God says what to do, that settles it for me."

"No problem," said the older man. "'I, too, am a prophet just like you, and at the Lord's command an angel told me to take you home with me and offer you my hospitality.' But the old prophet was lying."[14]

"You mean God has changed his mind? Well, as I always say, 'If God said it, I believe it.'" Thoroughly deceived, the trusting man from Judah went home with the older prophet.

But he lied to him.

The story has a sad ending and one might fairly ask, "Why is this story included in the Bible at all?" The younger prophet had no reason to suspect that the old man was lying. It would have been rude to suggest it. But he also had no reason to accept without question the contradiction of God's previous command. If only he had politely reserved his right to further investigate.

How often in these modern times we hear the claims of religious teachers that God, by his angels or his Spirit, has told them this or that. It would be rude to deny it. Besides, God has often spoken in this way. But God has also advised us to beware. *Prophets, too, can lie.*

Would You Buy Medicine from This Man?

An exciting moment in the frontier life of nineteenth century America was the arrival of the top-hatted traveling salesman with his wagon full of magic medicines. "Tell me what your ailment is, and I guarantee this will cure it!"

The testimonials of those who had been miraculously healed, coupled with the gullibility of the people, made the outlandish claims of the persuasive peddler seem quite believable. Surely his tonics were worth every penny that he asked!

But these claims are no more astounding than the ones made in the section on drugs in the Sears, Roebuck catalog of 1902. Quick relief is offered for ailments that modern medicine is still struggling to remedy. All come with Sears' absolute guarantee.

There is Sure Cure for the tobacco habit, the liquor habit, the opium and morphine habit, and obesity. There is Mexican Headache Cure, "positively guaranteed" to relieve splitting headaches within fifteen minutes. There are Dr. Rose's French Arsenic Complexion Wafers, "perfectly harmless" and guaranteed to make anyone beautiful, "no matter what your disfigurements may be." Dr. Hammond's Nerve and Brain Pills, "positively guarantee" to cure an endless list of ills, even poor memory. "No matter what the cause may be or how severe your trouble is, Dr. Hammond's Nerve and Brain Pills will cure you."

The hesitant customer is assured that all Sears' drugs have been prepared from prescriptions furnished by "the world's highest medical authorities," and he is warned to "beware of quack doctors who advertise to scare men into paying money for remedies which have no merit."

Sears, Roebuck would be the first today to urge its customers not to believe these incredible claims!

All around us, in the realm of religion, in the market-place, on the television screen, we are constantly confronted with competing claims. Obviously all of them cannot be true. We would do well to follow the apostle Paul's advice: "Test everything. Hold on to the good." [15]

No Shortcuts to Trust

The fact that the Bible invites inquiry, urges careful investigation and warns against being too easily persuaded — even by miraculous signs and wonders — speaks well of the trustworthiness of that book. Of course, even the Sears, Roebuck catalogue warns customers to beware of unreliable "quacks." But I could not trust a religious movement, teacher, or book that discouraged — or worse, forbade — sincere and thorough questioning of basic beliefs.

When a teacher of religion seems threatened by respectful but penetrating questions in his class, becomes increasingly defensive, even angry, as the students continue to press, there may be reason to suspect that the teacher's own positions lack adequate evidence — and all this undermines trust.

Trust can be quickly destroyed. And there are no shortcuts to its restoration. Claims of trustworthiness prove nothing.

Hitler claimed he could be trusted. When Satan questioned the genuineness of Job's faith, God did not settle the matter by divine pronouncement. Instead, he permitted the painful demonstration of the facts in the case. This is God's way of establishing the truth.

Even though God has been falsely accused of being unsafe to trust, there is only one way to meet the charge. Only by the demonstration of trustworthiness over a long period of time and under a great variety of circumstances — especially difficult ones — can trust be re-established and confirmed. The Bible — all sixty-six books — is a record of that demonstration.

The Authority of Truth

On the Sunday after Jesus was crucified, as two of his discouraged followers were walking home to Emmaus, trust was being severely tried. They were confused by the death of their Leader, for they "had hoped that he would be the one who was going to set Israel free." [16]

Jesus joined them on the way, but somehow they did not recognize him. The two men had serious questions that surely deserved the Lord's answers. But he did not reveal who he was. Instead he took them through the Old Testament, the record of the "many and various ways" in which God had spoken "by the prophets." I wish I could have heard the stories and statements he chose. Finally the two men recognized that their questions had been answered — all without knowing that it was the Lord himself who was leading them through the Scriptures.

Why didn't Jesus tell them who he was? In their reverence for him, they would gladly have accepted his every explanation. "If Jesus says it, we believe it, and that settles it!"

I believe that's why Jesus remained disguised. He did not

want them to run the risk of accepting what he said, just on the authority of his personal testimony. He could have been Satan in disguise, the one who "masquerades as an angel of light." [17]

Not until the two men had been led to an intelligent confidence based on adequate evidence was Jesus satisfied. Then, and then only did he reveal who he was.

Evidently God does not want us to believe what he says just because of who he is, the sovereign Creator of the universe. He wants us to trust him because of the kind of Person we have found him to be. He wants us to trust him in the light of the truth.

sn't there a danger that all this emphasis on friendship with a friendly God will undermine proper reverence?" The question came from a pastor at a church conference I attended recently, and I have heard others express the same concern.

The question surely deserves to be taken seriously, for many seem to find it difficult to revere God as both infinite Creator and gentle Friend. As the people demonstrated at the foot of Sinai, when the fear is gone, when there is no display of majesty and power, reverence seems to fade away. So long as the lightning flashed and the ground shook beneath their feet, the Israelites were prepared to promise God anything. Some might regard such trembling submission as "proper reverence." But not many days after the thunder had died away, the people were dancing wildly around a gold image of a calf![1]

As long as Jesus miraculously fed the crowds, healed the sick, and raised the dead, the people were ready to worship him and crown him king. But when he answered his enemies with

There is no need to be afraid."

such gentleness, when he treated sinners with such patience and respect, when he explained that his kingdom would not be set up by force, when on Calvary he humbly submitted to so much abuse, most of his followers either left or scoffed at his claim to be the Son of God.

Judas was one of those who mistook graciousness for weakness. When Jesus knelt to wash his feet, Judas despised him for his humility. The god Judas could respect would never degrade himself in such a manner.

Which inspires you to greater reverence: the terrifying manifestation of God's power on Mount Sinai or the picture of the great Creator quietly weeping on the Mount of Olives? If the story of Sinai and the story of Olivet have led us to see God as both majestic King and gracious Friend, then we have learned how to worship God with the kind of reverence he desires — reverence without fear, the reverence of friends.

Such friends can have a clearer understanding of God's ways, for he is able to speak to them more plainly. Unlike merely submissive servants, they are eager to know more about the one they admire. Jealous for God's reputation — as friends should be — they have shown they can be trusted with information others might misunderstand or even abuse.

To them God can reveal his gentleness, without danger of their despising it as weakness. He can tell them that he values nothing higher than their freedom, without danger of lessening their respect for discipline and order. He can show that he is forgiveness personified, without danger that they will take sin less seriously. He can assure them there is no need to be afraid, without danger of diminishing their reverence and awe.

Jesus minced no words in warning of the hazards of sharing such precious information with those who are not ready or able to receive it, or who may even find it offensive. As he neared the end of his marvelous depiction of God in the Sermon on the Mount, he solemnly advised, "Do not give what is holy to dogs; and do not throw your pearls before swine, or they will trample them under foot and turn and maul you."[2] If this should seem too strongly stated, the treatment Jesus received during the next three years proved the truthfulness of his warning.

No "Dark Speech" Between Friends

Imagine hearing God say that he can talk to you in ways that he cannot speak to other people, because you are his friend. Moses received this high compliment, and I have wondered how he must have felt as he listened to God explaining to Miriam and Aaron that he could speak more clearly to their brother than he could even to prophets.

Miriam and Aaron had become jealous of the special relationship Moses enjoyed with God, even though Moses himself is described as "very humble, more so than anyone else on the face of the earth."[3] I can recall thinking as a child that if Moses wrote that verse himself, it was not very humble of him to boast about his own humility! But later I came to realize that it takes a good deal of humility to admit to being meek. Meekness is rarely admired or trusted in a leader. During a presidential election, candidates do not extol their exceptional meekness and humility as especially qualifying them for high office!

One of the first poems my mother taught me began with the words, "Gentle Jesus, meek and mild, look upon this little child." I thought it was very beautiful at the time. I still do. But many of the people Jesus came to tell about his Father despised and rejected him for his gentleness, just as the prophet Isaiah had predicted they would.[4]

Centuries before, God had told meek Moses that some day he would raise up a special prophet from among the people of

Israel, "a prophet like you."[5] Jesus recognized this prediction as referring to himself.[6] And Moses must have watched with increasing wonder and admiration as the Son of God dealt with all kinds of people, and especially his enemies, with such humility and grace.

Before Jesus went out to be crucified, Moses came to talk with him on the Mount of Transfiguration. The prophet Elijah joined them, and all three — two men and their Creator God, though now in human form — talked "face to face," as friends speak with each other. Luke says they talked about the cruel rejection and execution Jesus was about to endure.[7]

Though so many despised Jesus for his meekness, do you suppose Moses was ashamed to stand there with his Lord? What an honor to be identified with "gentle Jesus, meek and mild!" Moses had not been ashamed to describe himself in the book of Numbers as more meek and humble "than anyone else on the face of the earth." To be that kind of a person is to be like God.

It would appear, though, that these qualities in Moses had not commanded the respect of his brother and sister. God summoned all three of them into his presence. Aaron and Miriam were ordered to step forward. And God said, *Hear my words:*

> *When there are prophets among you,*
> > *I the Lord make myself known to them in visions;*
> > *I speak to them in dreams.*
> *Not so with my servant Moses;*
> > *he is entrusted with all my house.*
> *With him I speak face to face — clearly, not in riddles;*
> > *and he beholds the form of the Lord.*

Why then were you not afraid to speak against my servant Moses?[8]

(The *King James Version* translates the Hebrew word for "riddles" as "dark speeches.")

Notice that God still addresses his friend Moses as his servant. On an earlier occasion God was described as speaking to Moses "face to face, as one speaks to a friend."[9] But friendship with God is not the end of service. *Jesus himself set the example of being a serving friend.*

Talking Plainly about the Father

Soon after Jesus made the offer of friendship recorded in John 15:15, he told the disciples that soon he would begin talking to them more clearly about the Father. He explained that up to this time he had been speaking to them in figures of speech, metaphors, parables — the "dark speech" he had not needed to use with his friend Moses. "The hour is coming when I will no longer speak to you in figures, but will tell you plainly of the Father."[10]

How soon did that hour arrive? The disciples apparently thought, at once. After Jesus had completed a brief but most significant statement about the Father, the disciples responded, "Yes, now you are speaking plainly, not in any figure of speech!"[11] Compare the Lord's words just a moment later, foretelling how the disciples would desert him, "The hour is coming, indeed it has come . . ."[12]

Jesus made his plain statement in the Aramaic language. John translated it into Greek. We read it in translations of John's translation. But we needn't worry that in all this translating, something of the original meaning may have become obscured.

The many versions of this passage read essentially the same. Here is the English of the *New International Version*:

> *Though I have been speaking figuratively, a time is coming when I will no longer use this kind of language but will tell you plainly about my Father. In that day you will ask in my name. I am not saying that I will ask the Father on your behalf. No, the Father himself loves you because you have loved me and have believed that I came from God. I came from the Father and entered the world; now I am leaving the world and going back to the Father.*[13]

I especially enjoy *Knox's* version of verse 27. "Because the Father himself is your friend, since you have become my friends..." Monsignor Knox translated from the Latin translation of John's translation Greek. But both in Latin and in Greek, the words for "love" and "friend" come from the same basic root.

In what Jesus said about the Father, is there anything that seems to be stated more clearly and less figuratively than before? I find only the simple words, which may be put in simple English, "I do not say to you that I will ask the Father for you, for the Father loves you himself."

Goodspeed translates this passage, "I do not promise to intercede with the Father for you, for the Father loves you himself."

As friends of a friendly God, the disciples were encouraged to present their own requests directly to the Father. It was not necessary for Jesus to do this for them.

They were, however, to "ask in my name," Jesus said. This was not to suggest that if God did not hear the name of his Son, he would be less willing to grant requests. The mention of the name of Jesus expresses grateful recognition that if the Son of

God had not shown us the truth about his Father, we would not know how we could approach him. We might not even want to.

In this sense, we have indeed needed someone to "mediate," to "intercede," to "intervene," all Latin-based words meaning respectively "to be in the middle," "to go between," "to come between." Every time we pray in Jesus' name, we thank God for Christ our Mediator, who came to bridge the gap between us and God and bring us the truth about our loving heavenly Father.

Because of Jesus, we know that we can talk with our heavenly Father "as one speaks with a friend." There is no need for some other friend between, for God himself is our Friend.

Of all that Jesus might have made plain about his Father, why did he choose this particular information, and why at this moment just before his crucifixion? Was this something the disciples would especially need to remember as they witnessed the events of the next few hours? Was it something the disciples needed to know very clearly, lest they misunderstand the meaning of his sacrificial death?

The Mystery of the Disappearing "Not"

Surprisingly, not everyone is pleased to hear this clear statement about the Father recorded in John 16. In fact, I once heard a minister denounce it as "damnable heresy." "If Jesus is not pleading for us with the Father," he went on, "we have no hope of being saved."

I'm sure this minister did not realize that he was condemning the words of Christ himself. So in all fairness I should point out that he is accustomed, as are many others, to reading John 16:26 without the all-important word "not." Jesus said, "I do *not* say to you that I will ask the Father on your behalf." But for many readers, the "not" has somehow disappeared.

On numerous public occasions, and sometimes even in print, I have seen this verse quoted — without the "not" — as a promise that Jesus will indeed plead with the Father for us. Some have expressed great surprise when their attention is called to the missing word. I have even heard preachers confess that, if the "not" really belongs, they don't know what to do with this text. Some simply ignore it.

One teacher explained, "Since we all know that Christ actually is interceding with the Father, John 16:26 is a difficult paradox." He meant this, of course, with the Lord's "not" still in place. But Jesus didn't say this statement was difficult. He said it was plain and clear!

A Chance to Ask Questions

The disciples missed another opportunity to act like friends as they had been invited, and raise questions the way friends do. They could well have asked Jesus if he really meant what he had just told them.

"Are you saying that there is no need for you to pray the Father for us? Then why was Moses instructed to set up the whole priestly system at Sinai?"

"Wasn't it the special work of the high priest to intercede with God in behalf of sinners?"[14]

"Didn't Moses have to plead with God not to pour out his wrath on the misbehaving people?"

"Didn't Moses himself report that he succeeded in persuading God to change his mind?"

The disciples could have called Jesus' attention to the very words of Scripture: "Moses implored the Lord his God, and said . . . 'Turn from your fierce wrath; change your mind and do not bring disaster on your people.' . . . And the Lord changed his mind about the disaster that he planned to bring on his people."[15]

"Are you telling us, Lord, that even Moses misunderstood?"

In our own time, with the advantage of having read the book of Hebrews, we could raise a further question: "Jesus, if the work of the high priest represented the very work you came to do — and have continued to do since your return into the presence of the Father — why would you say that there is actually no need for you to intercede with God in our behalf? And in spite of this clear statement, why would such good friends of yours as John and Paul still describe you in their New Testament letters as the Advocate who pleads our cause in the courts of heaven?[16] Did even they misunderstand? Was John perhaps puzzled to hear you go on asking the Father to do things for the disciples, right after you had said that you wouldn't?"[17]

I wish John had asked Jesus to help him understand the implications of his plain statement about the Father. Then John would have recorded the priceless answer, and we could be reading it today. However, from the rest of Scripture, we can have some idea of how the Lord would have explained.

"I Haven't Come to Contradict Moses"

Jesus might well have begun by repeating what he said to the critics who accused him of contradicting the teachings of the sacred Scriptures. "Do not suppose that I have come to abolish or do away with the law or the prophets; I have not come to abolish but to complete and fulfill."[18]

Then, as was his custom when answering such questions, Jesus might have traced the history of the whole idea that God's children needed someone to stand between them and their heavenly Father. He could have reminded the disciples of how God came down on Sinai to speak to his people, of the measures he had to take to gain their attention, how in terror the people begged Moses not to let God speak to them directly any longer lest they be destroyed.

"You speak to us, Moses, and we will listen; but do not let God speak to us, or we will die."[19]

"You see," Jesus might have continued, "it was the people who wanted someone in between, someone they understood to be God's friend, who could stand between them and the God of whom they were so terrified.

"But you disciples know that I am the one who was there on Sinai. Are any of you afraid of me? I have asked you to be my friends. You know it's safe for you to sit and talk with me openly like this."

I Didn't Want Anyone in Between

Then Jesus might have gone on, sadly, "I would have loved to talk like this with my people there in the wilderness. I didn't want anyone to intercede between us, as if I really didn't love my own children. But they did not know me as you do. First they were so irreverent. Then they were so scared. I could not order them not to be afraid. As you disciples surely must understand, trust and friendship cannot be commanded. So until they knew me better, I agreed that Moses could be the mediator. They were not afraid of him, and he was not afraid of me.

"Of course, there was no one between me and Moses. He really knew me and was my friend. There was no one between me and my old friend Abraham when he talked so candidly about my plans for the people of Sodom. And there was no one between me and Job when he felt free to express his feelings so strongly. His counselors thought I'd be angry, but actually I was honored by his trust.

"And now," Jesus might have concluded, "I have come myself to be the one between — just as I told Moses I would. Many may misunderstand my purpose in coming. Many may even sincerely thank God for sending me, the gentle one, to stand between them and their offended heavenly Father — as if I were kinder than he.

"But you know who I really am. You have seen that Isaiah was right when he foretold that the Prince of peace would actually be God.[20] Now tell me the truth, my disciples. Do you need anyone to protect you from me? Then you do not need anyone to protect you from the Father. When you were behaving so badly during supper, was there anyone between you and God when I washed your dirty feet? And I want you to remember in the future, that when I washed the feet of Judas, there was no one between him and his God.

"I have told you as plainly and clearly as I can that the Father loves you as much as I do. He is just as friendly and forgiving as I hope you have found me to be. He would even be just as willing to kneel and wash your dirty feet.

"But now I must go to be crucified. I want you to be with me on Calvary. I want you to watch me die. Perhaps it will help you understand more clearly what I have been trying to tell you about the Father."

Sadly, of the twelve disciples, John was the only one there. But he recorded what he heard and saw.

Who Loves Us More — Jesus or the Father?

At family worship years ago, when my youngest daughter was only six, we were reading together the children's story from a Christian magazine. It told dramatically how Jesus stands before his Father and asks him to forgive — especially little children who haven't been good!

"Daddy," interrupted Alice, with a troubled look on her face, "does this mean that God doesn't love us as much as Jesus does?" It seemed clear to her that the one who did the asking must be more loving than the one who had to be begged.

Worship was a bit longer that evening. A little girl had felt free to raise a very important question about God. And she really wanted to understand.

I told her the story of what Jesus had tried to make so plain and clear to his disciples in the upper room.

Now Alice explains to my grandchildren that God loves them just as much as Jesus does.

7 FRIENDSHIP AND GOD'S USE OF LAW

f you could ask God just one question, what would it be?

"I'd ask him to make me rich!" giggled a pretty teenager, as she stood with her friends outside Barry's butcher shop in England. "How to find a cure for cancer," "How to make everybody well," were the choices of two others.

"Is there one question you'd like to ask?" I inquired of the busy butcher himself.

"Yes. I'd like to ask God why, if he's so powerful, he doesn't feed the hungry people of Ethiopia." But Barry had already told of his disillusionment with a god who never seemed to do anything to help. "So I really don't believe in him anymore."

I talked with a man in a village nearby who still was a firm believer. "What question would you like to ask God—especially if you could ask only one?"

"I would ask him please to spell out more precisely what he wants me to do and how he wants me to do it."

Sharing a quadrangle bench at Cambridge University, I visited with a scholar who makes no secret of his great admiration for God. "What one question would you like to ask God?"

"I'm sick and tired of being told what I have to do."

"I know he's already answered this," he began. "But I'd like to hear him explain even more clearly why he has chosen to do things the way he has. Was there really no other way? And if so, why?"

In recent years, several religious polls have included this query about the most important question people would like to ask God. The responses have ranged from requests for material things — especially instant health and instant wealth — to most thoughtful inquiries about God himself.

The questions the disciples asked often reflected their selfish concerns, such as which of them was the greatest.[1] They were still arguing about this during their last supper with Jesus before he was crucified![2]

On an earlier occasion, two of them, who were brothers, had presumed to ask the Son of God if, in his coming kingdom, they could sit beside him in the most honored positions. They even brought their mother with them to intercede, to help persuade the Lord to give them the answer they wanted.[3] The request was not granted, but the other disciples were angry with the two brothers. Not that they were above making such a request for themselves!

What Would You Have Asked?

If you could have been with Jesus and his disciples that last night in the upper room, and you could have asked the Lord one question, what would it have been?

If Paul had been there, I wonder what question he might have asked. A few years later, in his epistle to believers in Galatia, he posed a question that would have been so appropriate for one of the disciples to raise that last night in the upper room. Paul's question was, "Why then the law?"[4]

Many of us have joined with Paul in considering this question. We love what Jesus said about freedom, friendship, love and trust. We also know from experience that none of these things can be commanded. Why, then, did God make so much use of law? Why would he order his children to love him and love each other — under threat of dire consequences if they failed to obey. Isn't this much more likely to produce trembling, sullen or even rebellious servants, rather than loyal and understanding friends? Why would God choose to run such risk?

Some of us also enjoy what Jesus said about speaking plainly and clearly. There is so much "dark speech" when people talk about God and salvation. But if God prefers simplicity and understanding, why did he tell Moses to establish such a complicated system of ceremonies and sacrifices, with all the strange symbols and figures of speech. Isn't all this mystery and pomp more likely to increase the distance between the Father and his children and make it more difficult for them to think and talk about him clearly? Why would God be willing to run this risk?

In his letter to the Galatians, Paul offers an answer to his own question. "Why then the law? It was added because of transgressions."[5] This is the translation of the *New International* and the *New Revised Standard* versions.

But the Greek word translated "because of" can also mean "for the purpose of." So the *Good News Bible* says that the law was added "in order to show what wrongdoing is." And the *Revised English Bible* explains that "it was added to make wrongdoing a legal offense."

One thing seems clear. If God's people had not been misbehaving, there would have been no need for the added law. As was explained to young pastor Timothy, "laws are made, not for good people, but for lawbreakers and criminals, for the godless and sinful, for those who are not religious or spiritual, for those who kill their fathers or mothers, for murderers, for the immoral, for sexual perverts, for kidnappers, for those who lie and give false testimony or who do anything else contrary to sound doctrine."6

Phillips translates, "The Law is not really meant for the good man, but for the man who has neither principles nor self-control."

God added the law because he knew we needed it.

How Can One Find the Right Meaning?

Even after Paul became a friend of God, he still was accustomed to using more than a little "dark speech" in his theological explanations — though not as dark, in my opinion, as it may appear in some translations.

Following his remarkable display of eloquence and erudition at the nearby city of Athens,7 Paul informed the believers in Corinth that from then on he was going to speak plainly and simply when he talked about God.8 Even so, the apostle Peter observed — very respectfully — that Paul's letters contained "some obscure passages, which the ignorant and unstable misinterpret."9

For this reason, when reading Paul's writings, I believe it is particularly important to read whole sections at a time, even whole letters or "books," in order to give Paul a fair chance to make plain his intent.

Paul's consistent emphasis is on the truth about God that is the basis for peace and freedom, love and trust, a trust like that of God's friend Abraham. Paul is now well aware that such precious things are not produced by might or power, as God told the prophet Zechariah. Nor can they be enforced by law. They can only come in free response to the gentle but long-lasting persuasiveness of truth. In this same letter to the Galatians, Paul explains that such things as "love, joy, peace, patience, kindness, generosity, faithfulness, gentleness, and self-control" all are "the fruit of the Spirit." [10]

While the Spirit of Truth has patiently continued his work of enlightenment and conviction, God has used many and various measures to control and protect his children as they are given opportunity to learn the truth. He has especially made use of law.

Our "Attendant" on the Way to Christ

The law, Paul goes on to explain in Galatians 3, has served as a "custodian" (RSV), a "disciplinarian" (NRSV), or, in the old *King James Version*, "schoolmaster." It was "put in charge of us" (REB) "until Christ came" (NRSV), or "to lead us to Christ." (NIV)

In his *American New Testament*, Goodspeed leaves room for the various possible meanings of the Greek by the simple translation, "So the Law has been our attendant on our way to Christ . . . But now that faith has come, we are no longer in the charge of the attendant." [11]

Those who have grown up with the *King James Version* are accustomed to the explanation that "the law was our schoolmaster to bring us unto Christ." When the *King James* was first printed in 1611, the words "to bring us" were printed in italics, to indicate that they had been supplied. The Greek says simply, "the law was unto Christ." In what sense the law was "to Christ" must be learned from reading Paul's explanation in the surrounding verses and in the light of all the rest of Scripture.

"Schoolmaster" may be a somewhat misleading translation, depending on one's understanding of what a schoolmaster's duties include. At the boy's school I attended — named formally in Latin, *Schola Grammatica Watfordensis* — our teachers were called "masters." As our "schoolmasters," they not only taught us but also exercised very firm discipline. Their primary function, however, was to teach.

If Paul had meant us to understand that the law was added to serve primarily as our teacher, he would have used another word, such as *didaskalos*, the source of our English "didactic." The term Paul chose, however, is *paidagogos*. Since this is the source of our English word "pedagogue," you can see how it could easily lead to the translation "schoolmaster," the choice of most other English versions that appeared earlier than the *King James*, going clear back to Tyndale. In 1534 he spelled it "scolemaster." The *Catholic Rheims New Testament*, translated from the Latin in 1582, simply left it "pedagogue."

The Greek term *paidagogos*, literally "boy-leader," actually referred to an attendant, usually a slave, who was put in charge of children. One of his duties was to accompany boys to and from school, to protect them and keep them out of trouble. He was not the teacher. The teacher was at the school. When the children became old enough to act responsibly and look after themselves, they were no longer kept under such supervision — presumably because it wasn't needed.

Paul is explaining that God added the law to perform a service similar to that of the "child-leader." But which law did the apostle have in mind? God has given many laws. Which law was to be our attendant on the way to Christ? The moral? The ceremonial? Any other? Paul doesn't say.

But of one thing we may be sure. The God who gave all the laws is the one who made the offer of friendship in John 15:15.

Some say it is none of our business to even wonder why God would make so much use of law. That's the way servants tend to talk. But the Sovereign himself has invited us to understand, something friends want to do.

Failure to understand God's law can lead to the unthinking, rote obedience that God deplored in the book of Isaiah:

> . . . these people draw near
>   with their mouths
> and honor me with their lips,
> while their hearts are far from me,
> and their worship of me is a
>   human commandment
>   learned by rote.[12]

Compare the translation of the *Good News Bible:* "These people claim to worship me, but their words are meaningless, and their hearts are somewhere else. Their religion is nothing but human rules and traditions, which they have simply memorized."

In the Bible, the heart is often referred to as representing the inner man, the place where a person does his or her thinking, as well as the seat of emotions and attitudes. For example, the Gospel of Mark mentions that some scribes were "reasoning in their hearts."[13]

The prophet Jeremiah looked forward to the day when God would fulfill his promise: "I will put my law within them, and I will write it on their hearts."[14] When the law of Ten Commandments was given to Moses to be passed on to the people, God wrote the ten precepts on tablets of stone. If God wanted only blind, unthinking obedience from his people, he would hardly be promising to write his law on his people's hearts, their centers of reasoning and intelligence. He would simply leave it engraved there on the stone, to go on spelling out his requirements.

The apostle Paul was a man of considerable intelligence.

He was eager to understand and explain the meaning and purpose of all God's laws. As the friend of a friendly God, he knew he was free to raise the question, "Why then the law?"

The more Paul studied the Ten Commandments, the more he came to admire them and agree that they made good sense. He told the believers in Rome, "I delight in the law of God in my inmost self."[15] The law engraved on the stone was being written on his heart.

The Ultimate Purpose of the Ceremonial Law

What about all the laws of offering and sacrifice, the "dark speech" of ritual and ceremony? Are these to be included in Paul's explanation that the law was added to be "our attendant on the way to Christ" and his plainer, clearer representation of the truth about God?

Frequently Old Testament prophets explained that if all the performance of prescribed religious services did not result in the people coming to know God and being kinder to each other, all those sacrifices and ceremonies had failed to meet their purpose. They were not indicating that these activities should stop. It was God who had prescribed them. They were simply emphasizing that nothing was more important than the knowledge of God.

Speaking for God, Hosea wrote this message to the people:

> It is true love that I have wanted, not sacrifice;
> The knowledge of God rather than burnt-offerings.[16]

"I would rather have my people know me than have them burn offerings to me," is how the *Good News Bible* reads.

Jeremiah predicted that when God's law has been written on the hearts of people, "no longer shall they teach one another, or say to each other, 'Know the Lord,' for they shall all know me." [17]

In the Bible, the Hebrew and Greek words translated "know" can mean more than being merely acquainted or informed. Depending on the context, to "know" someone can imply an attitude of appreciation and approval, a relationship with someone who is specially valued. Paul told the Corinthians that "anyone who loves God is known by him." [18]

God knew Abraham, and Abraham knew him. This is why they could be such good friends. When God says he wants to be known by us, he is inviting us also to be his friends.

God's Laws Are No Threat to Friendship

Would you find it possible to be friendly with a god who imposed arbitrary laws, just to show his authority and test our willingness to obey? Would you want to know him? Would you want to live with such a god for eternity?

I recognize that some devoutly religious people believe it is important for God to impose at least a few arbitrary rules. How else could he know if we are obeying him or not, they say. Perhaps we're only doing what seems sensible and right.

If it's true that some laws really don't make sense, then there's no point in our trying to understand their meaning. We should just bow our heads and like unthinking servants, simply do what we're told.

Yes, I'm willing to bow my head. But I bow it in awe that our infinite Creator, who indeed has a perfect right to be arbitrary, has chosen instead to be just the opposite.

When a man bails out of his plane at 5000 feet, he doesn't have to release his parachute. There's no one there to make him do it. He could say to himself, "I'm sick and tired of being told what I have to do!" Here is his chance to show independence of the rules. But if he wants to live to fly again another day, it makes very good sense to release that parachute!

Consider the law of Ten Commandments. Some speak of those rules as if they were arbitrary restrictions of our freedom. But if we really kept those commandments, in the way Jesus demonstrated, in what respect would we be less free? James calls those rules "the royal law of liberty." [19]

Jesus and Paul agree with Moses that to keep the Ten Commandments means to love God with all your heart and your neighbor as yourself. Paul sums it up like this: "He who loves his neighbour has met every requirement of the law. The commandments, 'You shall not commit adultery, you shall not commit murder, you shall not steal, you shall not covet,' and any other commandment there may be, are all summed up in the one rule, 'Love your neighbour as yourself.' Love cannot wrong a neighbour; therefore love is the fulfilment of the law." [20]

To be sure that we understand what it means to love, Paul explains the meaning in his letter to the church in Corinth. "Love is patient; love is kind; love is not envious or boastful or arrogant or rude. It does not insist on its own way; it is not irritable or resentful; it does not rejoice in wrongdoing, but rejoices in the truth." [21]

Imagine living in a community where everyone behaves like this. Everyone can be trusted, no one ever takes advantage of anyone else, and women and children can safely walk the streets alone at any hour.

But consider further the tenth of the Ten Commandments. The words "You shall not covet" actually prohibit any kind of evil desire. Now imagine living in a community where people not only never do anything wrong; they don't even want to! No one has to order the people to stop lying, stealing, murdering, being impatient or selfishly insisting on having their own way. The Ten Commandments are not posted on any wall. Everyone is already convinced that it makes good sense to follow the way of life prescribed in those age-old rules.

Obedient Servant or Obedient Friend?

If you are a believer and are eager to do God's will, what makes you willing to obey?

Would you say, "I do what I do because God has told me to, and he has the power to reward and destroy"? Is this why you don't murder and commit adultery, because God has said you musn't? Are you saying that you might do it otherwise, but you can't afford to incur his displeasure?

This is the way a trembling servant talks. It might be all right for a beginner or a little child. But it suggests that God's laws are arbitrary and don't make good sense in themselves. This kind of obedience does not speak very favorably of God himself.

Would you rather say, "I do what I do as a believer because God has told me to, and I love him and want to please him"? Is this why you don't steal or tell lies? You see nothing wrong or harmful about doing these things. It is just that you want so much to please God. For some reason he does not like it when you steal or lie, and since he has been so generous, you feel under some obligation to please him. It would only be grateful and fair.

Again, this is all servant talk. And again, it might be all right for a beginner or little child. It might even be some progress beyond the obedience prompted only by fear of punishment and desire for reward. But it still implies an arbitrariness in God's commandments and doesn't speak very well of his character and government.

There is another possible approach to obedience. Could you say this? "I do what I do because I have found it to be right and sensible to do so, and I have increasing admiration and reverence for the one who so advised and commanded me in the days of my ignorance and immaturity. And being still somewhat ignorant and immature, I am willing to trust and obey the one whose counsel has always proved to be so sensible, when he tells me to do something beyond my present understanding."

This sounds more like the way an understanding friend would talk. And it speaks well of God, as an admirable, trustworthy Friend.

When God asked his friend Abraham to sacrifice his son, Abraham knew God well enough, first to recognize his voice, and then to obey at once so incredible a command. But on the long journey to the place of sacrifice, Abraham respectfully questioned, "Why?" As he thought it through in the light of his knowledge of God, he came to the conclusion that God would either provide a substitute or resurrect his son. God's old friend was right![22]

On the sad day that our Great Dane died, we comforted ourselves by bringing home an Old English mastiff puppy. Though she already weighs close to 150 pounds, she is still very much a pup, and her etiquette around the house needs considerable refinement. This is especially true in the garden, where Molly, as we named her, quickly developed a keen appetite for the large red flowers of the hibiscus bush.

Molly soon discovered that we were not at all pleased to watch her running around the pool with remnants of several of the beautiful blossoms hanging from her muzzle. Eventually it was established that she must not even touch those tempting flowers.

Molly is a very loving dog and seems most eager to please.

The obedience of a loving, well-trained dog.

She appears quite depressed when she senses that she has incurred our displeasure. This was apparently enough to keep her from breaking the rule. That is, as long as she thought we were looking! But when she saw us disappear into the house, she felt free to go right back and attack those lovely flowers.

When we observed this through one of the windows, we would hurry out and re-affirm that prohibition. We didn't have to repeat this often before Molly became aware that though she could not see us watching, whenever she disobeyed we would some-how suddenly reappear. Had she perhaps caught a glimpse of us behind the glass?

Only occasionally now do we see her at the hibiscus bush, sitting there on her wide haunches — but with only a glance at those tasty flowers. She is looking back over her shoulder, earnestly peering at each of the windows to see if we might be watching after all.

We are not expecting Molly to think this through and decide for herself that it doesn't make sense to destroy those flow-ers. It's enough that she obeys because she loves us and wants so much to please.

But surely it would be very disap-pointing to God, if his intelligent children should only give him the obedience of a lov-ing, well-trained dog.

Why Do You Brush Your Teeth?

When I was a boy, I shared a large bedroom with two of my brothers. Every night Mother would come to tuck us in. As she stood by my bed, she would often ask, "Did you say your prayers? Did you read your Bible? Did you wash your neck? Have you brushed your teeth?" If the answer was No, Mother would insist that the matter be taken care of before I went to sleep.

In those days, the main reason why I brushed my teeth was that Mother told me to. I loved her and wanted her approval. Besides, if I had shown a rebellious attitude, it might have meant another session at that bottom stair.

But now that I've grown up a bit, no one has to order me to brush my teeth. It makes such good sense to do so, and I know what happens when I don't. Whenever I visit the office of my friendly periodontist, I read again the irresistible message he has posted on his wall: "You only have to floss the teeth you want to keep."

If my mother could appear beside my bed tonight and ask those same questions again, do you think I'd grumble: "There we go, back under law?"

No. I'd love to hear her ask me again, "Graham, have you brushed your teeth?" I'd like to thank her for the years when she made us brush our teeth. That's why we still have some teeth to brush.

And I'd like to thank her for helping us understand why, in our ignorance and immaturity, God had to make so much use of law.

8 HOW SERVANTS AND FRIENDS LOOK AT SIN AND SALVATION

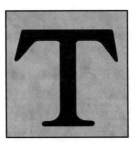he picture people have of God, and their understanding of his use of law, seem to affect significantly the way they look at sin and the plan of salvation.

My grandfather made no secret of his position on the subject of sin. He was clearly dedicated to its exposure and eradication. He also faithfully worked with people to prevent it — including with me.

More than 55 years have passed since I last talked with Grandpa, pacing back and forth together on his lawn, or sitting comfortably by the fire. But I can still remember the conversation returning from time to time to the subject of sin.

"'Sin is the transgression of the law,'" Grandpa would remind me, his beard adding solemnity to the sound of those venerable words from the *King James Version*.

"Yes, Grandpa. I remember that you told me that once before."

"And where do you find that verse in the Bible?" he would inquire.

"Very good, sir! If you say so, sir!"

"First John three, verse four," I would reply, to his satisfaction.

"Now, what law was John referring to?" Grandpa would continue. "Since, of course, it was the law of Ten Commandments, that means that sin is disobeying one of those ten rules."

Then Grandpa would repeat that serious verse from the book of James, " 'To him that knoweth to do good, and doeth it not, to him it is sin.'[1] And we know what happens to sinners, don't we?" Grandpa would begin his conclusion. "We know that unrepentant sinners will never enter into the Kingdom of Heaven."

My grandfather could have chosen to mention more horrifying things described in the Bible as the destiny of the disobedient. But he also believed in all the verses about God being love, and about Jesus saying that he wanted little children to come to him. So he chose to mention only that sinners would not be allowed to share in the joys of the hereafter.

I was very fond of my grandfather. He was kind and generous and would obviously rather die than sin. He was totally devoted to serving the Lord and anyone in need, the kind of neighbor you could live next door to and never bother to lock up your house. I hoped that when I grew up, I could be as good a man as my old grandpa.

Even when I was attending college six thousand miles away, my grandfather would write letters from time to time, each of them including instruction and exhortation designed to keep me from straying from the paths of righteousness.

A Larger View of Sin

It was there in college that I began trying to read and understand the Bible as a whole. And it helped to have some knowledge of the languages in which it was first written. I soon came to realize that the Bible doesn't always describe sin as just breaking the rules.

In that much-used definition in 1 John 3:4, the Greek word for "transgression of the law" may also be literally translated "lawlessness." This would indicate that sin is first a rebellious attitude or frame of mind, a hostility to God and to his law, that in turn may lead one to commit this or that act of disobedience. The 1989 *New Revised Standard Version* translates, "Everyone who commits sin is guilty of lawlessness; sin is lawlessness."

The Obedience That Comes from Trust

In the introduction to his letter to the believers in Rome, Paul states his conviction that he had been specially commissioned to bring about a new kind of obedience. It was to be different from the kind of obedience he himself had offered before he met Jesus on the Damascus road. It was to be what he calls literally "obedience of faith," "obedience of trust."

"Law-obedience" is what Paul used to practice with such zeal, and he was not at all pleased with the results. It had made him intolerant toward other people, even cruel. "Law-obedience" had actually led him to violate the whole spirit of God's law, the law of love.

By now urging "faith-obedience" or "trust-obedience," is Paul doing away with the law? "By no means!" Paul exclaims. "On the contrary, we uphold the law."[2] Phillips interprets, "We put the Law in its proper place."

One proper place for the law has been to serve as "our attendant on the way to Christ." But the ultimate place is the one Jeremiah described. Paul agrees with the prophet. What the law requires may be written on the heart — the place, Paul explains to the Romans, where the conscience is active and people do their thinking.[3]

"Trust-obedience" is the kind that results from "knowing" God, in the full meaning of that word. It comes from learning the truth about him and his use of law. It is the result of being won back to trust him as a Friend, to admire him for his wise and gracious ways.

This means that the Spirit of Truth has succeeded in writing the law "on our hearts." Now we freely do what the law requires, not because we've been ordered to, but because we're convinced in our own minds that what the law requires is right.

The Obedience That Comes From Conviction

To act without, or against, such conviction is sin, Paul seems to be saying to the Roman believers. "Anything which is not from faith is sin" is a literal translation of his words.[4]

One of the meanings of the word commonly translated "faith," "belief," or "trust" is "conviction." In the much-quoted definition of faith in Hebrews 11:1, faith is described as "conviction of things not seen," "conviction" being the literal meaning of the Greek.

From what Paul has just been discussing in chapter 14, it seems clear that in verse 23 he is using the word "faith" in the sense of "conviction." So the *New Revised Standard Version* translates, "Whatever does not proceed from faith is sin," with the footnote, "Or *conviction.*"

It doesn't seem difficult to understand how proceeding *against* one's convictions could be regarded as sin. It's not that the person who does something wrong like this is in legal trouble with God. But to violate one's conscience is to weaken the ability to discern between right and wrong. It means to be a person who lacks integrity and is not safe to trust.

This is not the behavior of a trusted friend. The cost of failing to follow one's convictions is very great.

But Paul seems to be warning that to proceed *without* personal convictions is also sinful and wrong. "Let all be fully convinced in their own minds," Paul urges in Romans 14. How could turning down this generous invitation be regarded as sin?

Failure to accept the freedom and responsibility of making decisions for oneself, and leaning on others for direction, leaves one increasingly vulnerable to harmful influence. Such a person becomes like the children Paul pictures as "tossed to and fro and blown about by every wind of doctrine."[5] He is like "a wave in the sea," James agrees with Paul, "driven and blown about by the wind . . . unable to make up his mind and undecided in all he does."[6]

Most seriously, like the helpless infant pictured in the book of Hebrews, his "faculties" have not been "trained by practice to distinguish good from evil."[7] Not having exercised his God-given ability to decide for himself, he has damaged that place where a man does his thinking, that place where the Spirit of Truth does his most essential work.

Such an unstable person is not safe to rely on as a trusted friend. Like the results of going *against* our personal convictions, the cost of not *forming* our own convictions is also very great.

The Sin of Moses at the Rock

Not long before the people of Israel crossed the Jordan into the Land of Canaan, God's good friend Moses committed a sin so serious that he was not permitted to go with them into the Promised Land.

Once again the people were in an uproar over lack of water. "Why have you brought us up out of Egypt, to bring us to this wretched place?" they complained. Moses and Aaron took the matter to the Lord.

"'Gather the assembly together,' the Lord instructed. 'Speak to that rock before their eyes and it will pour out its water.' "

Moses and Aaron gathered the assembly. But Moses did not follow the rest of the Lord's instructions. He still felt too provoked by the ungrateful grumbling of the people.

" 'Listen, you rebels,' " Moses cried angrily, " 'must we bring you water out of this rock?' Then Moses raised his arm and struck the rock twice with his staff. Water gushed out, and the community and their livestock drank.

"But the Lord said to Moses and Aaron, 'Because you did not trust in me enough to honor me as holy in the sight of the Israelites, you will not bring this community into the land I give them.' "8

Moses pleaded with God to reconsider. " 'Let me go over and see the good land beyond the Jordan.' " In fact, he pleaded so long that finally God had to say plainly to his old friend, " 'That is enough, . . . Do not speak to me anymore about this matter.' "9

Just before Moses went up on Mount Nebo to die, God reminded him of what it was about his and Aaron's behavior at the rock that was so seriously wrong — wrong enough, in fact, to justify denying them the well-earned reward for 40 years of faithful service. I wonder how Moses felt as he wrote this down for later generations to read.

" 'This is because both of you broke faith with me in the presence of the Israelites . . . and because you did not uphold my holiness among the Israelites.' "10

Moses had gone out of his way to protect God's reputation. Remember how he assured the people there was no need to be afraid of God. Remember the story of how he even ventured to advise God not to hurt his own reputation.

Now Moses had let God down. He had "broken faith." He had not allowed God to reveal himself to the people as he chose to be seen that day.

On the verge of entering Canaan, with all the dangers there, it was essential that the people trust God implicitly, or they would never survive. But at that moment there in the wilderness, the people were in a hostile, suspicious mood. How could God persuade them to change their minds and feel confident that he would look after them?

As Paul would explain in later years, it is the kindness of God that leads to repentance and trust.[11] God chose that day to give his undeserving people all the water they needed. No anger. No condemnation. No correction. Just a gushing stream of water.

I wish the record showed that the hearts of some people were touched. But Moses had confused what God was trying to say. By his anger and impatience, he had misrepresented God. Years before, the people had asked Moses to be their mediator, to stand between them and the wrath of God, and to be God's spokesman to them. If even meek Moses was so angry with them, God must be furious.

When the people learned that Moses had been banned from entering Canaan, they must have been puzzled by the severity of the punishment. "What do you suppose the old man did?" I can hear them wondering to each other. "And why doesn't he offer a sacrifice and ask for forgiveness? Then God could let him go in after all."

But God had already forgiven his old friend. Moses must have been horrified to realize the significance of what he had done. In imagination I can hear him cry, "God, I'm so sorry that I let you down. But please, God, can we still be friends?"

The Lord knew that treating his old friend so sternly would not be testing their friendship too far. He knew that Moses, as a friend, would understand. God had gone on record before the universe that there is nothing more serious than for friends to let each other down. There is no sin more damaging than for an influential leader to misrepresent the truth about God.

The Lord was with Moses on Mount Nebo when he died.[12] And he brought him back to talk face to face on the Mount of Transfiguration.[13] God and Moses are still good friends.

Understanding Sin as a Legal Problem

The idea that sin should be understood as a breach of faith, a breakdown of trust, is not of primary concern to servants — that is, to servants as Jesus depicted them in John 15:15.

Servants, he explained to his disciples, "do not know their master's business." They feel it is none of their business to understand what their master is doing. Their duty is to do what they're told, and obey the rules — whether they agree with them or not.

Believers who think and act like such servants tend to be preoccupied with their legal standing with their Lord and Master, how to please him, and how to stay out of trouble. Sin is seen primarily as the breaking of the rules.

It is their understanding that by committing such transgression they will incur the wrath of God and find themselves in serious legal trouble. Unless something is done to remove their guilt, legal penalties will be imposed. And for the slightest infraction of the rules, the penalty is nothing less than painful execution — or even eternal torture.

Some servant-believers are so accustomed to this kind of government that they fervently defend it, all in the name of justice, as they understand that term. They will concede that in civilized courts of law, justice never justifies torture. But in God's government?

"Well," the servant says, "who are you to question his inscrutable ways? As a good and faithful servant, just bow your head and believe. Such fearsome treatment at the hands of God is not only the right but also the loving thing to do."

I heard someone say this again just the other day. He was the kind of believer who surely qualifies as a "good and faithful servant."

"God," he went on to explain, "is required by law, by justice, and by the holiness of his own character and government, not only to destroy those who oppose his will, but first to painfully punish them for an appropriate length of time."

When I asked him how he could consider such inhuman punishment the loving thing to do, he replied, "Don't you believe the Scriptures? The Bible says God is love. That means that even if it doesn't make sense to us, anything God does must be the loving thing to do." It made me think again of that famous bumper sticker.[14]

"Your God is Too Kind"

I have heard servants sometimes charge that friends lack a keen sense of justice. They do not leave room in their understanding of God for just and essential punishment. Their God is simply too weak and kind. "You have a marshmallow God," I heard one servant say.

The truth is precisely the opposite. Friend-believers have great concern about righteousness, which is the literal meaning of the Greek word often translated "justice." The English word "justice" comes from the Latin translation of the Greek.[15]

Friends admire God's righteousness and would love to be like him. And to do what is right is, of course, to do what is just. But servants tend to think of justice in terms of retribution and punishment.

"I find comfort in the thought that some day God will bring

retribution on those who have hurt me so much," I heard a believer say. "Now, I'm not asking for vengeance, you understand. I'm just asking for justice."

Recently, a serial killer, who had been incredibly cruel, was sentenced to death by electrocution. As the hour for his execution approached, a crowd gathered outside the prison. And some very religious people were heard to cry, "Burn, Bundy, burn!"

Afterwards, some of them complained that it was not fair that Bundy should burn such a little while. Justice had not really been satisfied. But they comforted themselves with the thought that someday, at the hands of God, justice would fully be done. Bundy would burn for eternity.

Destruction Does Not Discipline the One Destroyed

Friends understand the need for punishment. They know that God disciplines those whom he loves. Discipline is for the purpose of correction and instruction, and friends trust God to discipline them when they need it. And they do not chafe under such discipline, as servants are more likely to do. They know that God's discipline is always for their best good. "Thank you, God, I needed that," is the grateful response of a friend.

But destruction is not discipline. *Destruction does not discipline the one destroyed.* And to prolong the pain of the execution teaches him nothing. His life is done.

Then would God extend the suffering to say something to the ones looking on? Will saints in the kingdom, as they watch the agony of the lost, be saying to their heavenly Father, "Thank you, God, we needed that. Justice demanded that they be punished like this, and we needed to watch it happen. Besides, if that's what you really do to sinners, you can count on us to be very obedient for the rest of eternity!"

That's the obedience that comes from fear, the obedience

of trembling servants who simply do what they're told. It would not be the free cooperation of understanding friends, that God so much desires. And what do you think God's friends would be saying as they watched the wicked die?

The Servant View of Salvation

In the servant's understanding of sin and its divinely imposed penalty, salvation is seen as God's merciful provision by which the guilty servant's legal standing may be adjusted and he will not have to be executed after all.

How the death of an innocent substitute makes this adjustment possible is of no serious concern to the servant. All he wants to know is whether his Master is satisfied and his righteous anger about the sinner's misbehavior has somehow been assuaged — or "propitiated."

Special Words

Do you know the meaning of that word "propitiated"? Years ago my oldest daughter came home from Bible class repeating the verse to be memorized that week. It was Romans 3:25, as translated in the *King James Version*.

"'Whom God hath set forth to be a propitchiation through faith in his blood,'" she began.

"That's not pronounced 'propitchiation,'" I interrupted. "It's 'propitiation,' as if the first two syllables were spelled p-r-o-p-i-s-h."

"No it isn't, Daddy," Lorna replied with unquestionable certitude. "My teacher says it's pronounced 'propitchiation.'"

"Very well," I conceded for the moment, "but tell me now, what does the word 'propitchiation' mean?"

"Oh, we don't have to know that, Daddy. All we have to do is memorize the verse. Then we get a gold star on our record."

It reminded me of the story sometimes told of the woman

who informed her pastor that there was one word in the Bible that especially inspired her soul.

"What word might that be?" the pastor inquired.

"Oh," she replied, with face aglow, "it's that wonderful word Mesopotamia!"[16]

One of the characteristics of the servant view of sin and salvation is the frequent use of terms and phrases that friends might consider "dark speech." Such terms as "justification," "sanctification," "expiation," and, of course, "propitiation."

It may help to remember that these actual words were never used by the writers of the Bible. Even Paul never used the word "justification," for which he is so well-known. That's a Latin-based English word. Paul wrote his epistles in Greek. And the Greek can be translated into more simple language than you find in some of the versions. Recent translations into many languages around the world have gone a long way toward making the words of the Bible more plain and clear.

Sacred Phrases

Such familiar old phrases as "washed in the blood," "there's power in the blood," "covered by his righteousness," "accepted in the Beloved," "saved by the blood of the Lamb," and so many more, surely qualify as "dark speech." This does not in any way suggest that their meaning is not of great importance. But what do these phrases mean?

Try explaining to a child who has just had the blood washed from his wounded knee, what it means to be "washed in the blood of the Lamb." I believe it is a significant test of our own understanding to explain sin and salvation to a little child.

In religion class one day, I asked a medical student to explain why he thought Jesus had to die. "Because 'without shedding of blood is no remission,'" he replied without a moment's hesitation, quoting that famous verse in the book of Hebrews, as translated in the *King James Version*.[17] Then he settled back in his chair, as if nothing more could be said.

"But does that mean," I persisted, "that if blood had not been shed, God could not have forgiven sinners?"

"Why can't you accept the Bible just the way it reads?" he replied with some agitation. "Why do you have to confuse things by always asking for the meaning?"

Isn't that the way servants talk?

The View of God's Friends

The fact that God's friends are not so preoccupied with their legal standing does not mean that they take sin lightly. Precisely the opposite is true! Whereas servants are concerned about breaking the rules, friends are concerned about anything that would undermine trust and damage their relationship with God. Most of all, they are concerned about anything that would in any way misrepresent God — whether or not the details have been spelled out in any law.

Friends understand salvation as the healing of the damage sin has done. And sin's damage, if not healed, is nothing less than fatal. Disorderly, irresponsible behavior, if persisted in, can totally destroy the capacity for trust and trustworthiness.

To the servant, what makes sin most dangerous is that it angers God.

To the friend, what makes sin most dangerous is what it does to the sinner. To persist in sin is to destroy oneself.

Sin Is Like Poison

If you should find it necessary to keep some potent poison at your house, where would you put it? Where the children could readily find it? Or on the highest shelf in the garage?

"You absolutely must not touch that poison," you warn the children. "Don't even go near that shelf. If you disobey me, you'll be severely punished."

Some time later you hear an ominous crash. You rush out to the garage, and there on the floor is your son, the broken bottle beside him.

What would you do to your dying child? He has disobeyed you. Would it occur to you even for a moment that he should be put to death for his sin? He's dying already.

You know that the poison works quickly. You don't have much time. Would you waste precious moments scolding him for his disobedience? Would you insist that he repent and tell you he's sorry. Would forgiveness keep him from dying?

You run to fetch the antidote. But your son refuses to take it, and you sadly watch him die.

What caused his death? You loved him. You forgave him. You offered him the antidote. But he still died.

Friends don't see sin as a legal problem. They see it as working like poison. And they understand the plan of salvation as God's offer of the antidote.

But what if we refuse the antidote? What happens to those who turn down the offer of salvation?

he prophet Hosea be-
gins his book by telling
the story of God asking him to do something that he must have
found almost unbelievable. God asked him to marry a woman
who behaved like a prostitute. If she wasn't acting promiscuously
like this already, God knew she soon would be.

Now, this is not the kind of direction God included in his
laws for daily living. It is not a command that obviously makes
such good sense that one would go on doing it anyway, even if
God never asked again.

This was a unique command, like the one to Abraham. God
had something of great importance he wanted to say to his people,
and he asked his friend Hosea not only to convey the message,
but also to demonstrate its meaning.

Since Hosea knew God very well, as shown by the rest of
his book, he obeyed the command and married Gomer. They had
three children. Depending on how you read the story, perhaps
only one of them was his. Later she left him to live with other
lovers.

"I forgive you."   "God, does that mean I'm finished with what you want to
say?" Hosea may have wondered.

"No, the most important part is still to come. Now go and find your wife. Take some money with you in case you have to buy her back. When you find her, see if you can persuade her to come home and be your faithful wife from now on."

So Hosea went to look for his wife. And I have imagined him going from place to place asking, "Have you seen Gomer?"

He finally found her. If you had been in Hosea's place, what would you have said to your wife? If you loved her, would you have condemned her for what she was doing? Would you have grabbed her and tried to drag her home? If so, do you think she would have wanted to live with you again? If she had absolutely refused to come, would you have been willing to give her up and let her go?

In the emotion of the moment, could you have said anything? Except, perhaps, "Please come home."

"Are you sure you want me to?"

"Yes." Or maybe just a tearful nod.

Whatever it was that Hosea did, Gomer went home with him.

How God Feels About His Promiscuous People

The story of the prophet and his wife seems to represent the relationship between God and his faithless people. For a long time God had tried to persuade rebellious Israel to come back and trust him again and behave like trustworthy people. But though they were the children of his best friend Abraham, they mocked his love and spurned his every advance.

Since trust can not be won by force, what else could God do but sadly give them up and let them go? But without his protection, the results would be disastrous.

Sorrowfully God recalls the long centuries of frustrated love.

When Israel was a child, I loved him
      and called him out of Egypt as my son.
But the more I called to him,
      the more he turned away from me.
My people sacrificed to Baal;
      they burned incense to idols.
Yet I was the one who taught Israel to walk.
I took my people up in my arms,
      but they did not acknowledge that I took
         care of them.
I drew them to me with affection and love.
      I picked them up and held them to my cheek;
      I bent down to them and fed them.

They refuse to return to me, and so they must return to Egypt, and Assyria will rule them. War will sweep through their cities and break down the city gates. It will destroy my people because they do what they themselves think best. They insist on turning away from me. They will cry out because of the yoke that is on them, but no one will lift it from them.

How can I give you up, Israel?
      How can I abandon you? Could I ever destroy you
         as I did Admah,[1]
      or treat you as I did Zeboiim?[2]
My heart will not let me do it!
      My love for you is too strong.[3]

Phillips translates the first two lines of verse 8:

"How, oh how, can I give you up, Ephraim!
How, oh how, can I hand you over, Israel!

119

Paul Must Have Read Hosea

The apostle Paul, as a well-educated Jew, had often read the writings of Hosea. I wonder how he felt about this description of what God does to those who refuse him. Is it possible that the memory of this passage was part of what was troubling his conscience as he set out on the Damascus road to do such violence to people he thought were rejecting God?

At least, when it came his turn to write on the subject, Paul explained three times at the beginning of his letter to the Romans that God "gave up" and "handed over" people he could not reach with the truth.

> For the wrath of God is revealed from heaven against all ungodliness and wickedness of those who by their wickedness suppress the truth. For what can be known about God is plain to them, because God has shown it to them.

> Ever since the creation of the world his eternal power and divine nature, invisible though they are, have been understood and seen through the things he has made. So they are without excuse; for though they knew God, they did not honor him as God or give thanks to him, but they became futile in their thinking, and their senseless minds were darkened.

> Claiming to be wise, they became fools; and they exchanged the glory of the immortal God for images resembling a mortal human being or birds or four-footed animals or reptiles.

> Therefore God gave them up in the lusts of their hearts to impurity, to the degrading of their bodies among themselves, because they exchanged the truth about God for a lie and worshiped and served the creature rather than the Creator. . . .

> For this reason God gave them up to degrading passions. . . .

> And since they did not see fit to acknowledge God, God

gave them up *to a debased mind and to things that should not be done.*[4]

How consistent this is with the picture of a God who wants the love and cooperation of understanding friends. Notice that God is not described as punishing people by darkening their minds. Their minds became dark and senseless as a natural result of their suppression and rejection of the truth. They had "exchanged the truth about God for a lie" and had even begun worshipping animals. Some people those days even worshipped beetles and crocodiles!

Since it is a law that we tend to become like the things we worship and admire, imagine the effect of worshipping a beetle. "Dear Lord Beetle," the children might pray. "Bless Mummy, bless Daddy, and help us to be more like you."

At the beginning of his explanation of what God does to those who refuse the offer of salvation, Paul speaks of God's wrath.

This is evidently not like human anger, for notice how God shows his wrath. Paul agrees with Hosea: What God does to those who do not want him is to tell them of his love and disappointment and then sadly let them go.

When people persist in rejecting God and suppressing the truth, what else can he do but give them up and leave them to the inevitable consequences of their senseless thinking and rebellious choice?

But how serious are the consequences when God gives us up and lets us go? Could they even be fatal? And if so, why?

Doctors Don't Kill Patients Who Won't Cooperate

Imagine yourself in the office of a physician. He is a renowned specialist in the treatment of your particular condition.

As he hands you a bottle of the special antidote for your disease, you seem to hesitate a moment.

"Doctor," you ask anxiously, "what *is* it that you do to patients who won't take their medicine?"

"Why are you looking so worried?" he replies. "And what do you mean by asking, 'What *is* it that you do?' Have people been talking about how I treat my patients?"

"Yes, doctor, and that's why I'll admit I'm a little scared. There's another doctor, who must be no friend of yours, who says that you . . ."

But you hesitate to go on. The physician seems so professional and has such a friendly face. He invites you to continue.

"What I was going to tell you, doctor, is that some people say that if patients won't take their medicine, you punish them severely. Even torture them. Even kill them. They say that you do this to discourage other patients from wasting your precious time. And I suppose it does help them pay their bills more promptly."

"Then why have you come to my office?"

"Well, I've tried everyone else, and no one's been able to help me. I hear that you've had the most success in treating my problem, so I thought coming to see you would be worth running the risk."

The doctor seems quite understanding. "All I can say is, please take your medicine. And I want you to take it exactly as prescribed. Your condition is so serious that if you don't let me help you, you won't live much longer."

Doctors don't kill patients who won't cooperate. But sometimes they have to watch them die. And sometimes even doctors cry.

Sometimes the dying patient is the doctor's own child. As both father and physician, he has tried hard to persuade his son

"What is it that you do to patients who won't take their medicine?"

122

to change his self-destructive way of life. The son has steadily refused, and a loving father has no choice but to let him go. Now all the father-physician can do is stand by the bedside and watch his child die.

Can the Heavenly Physician Be Trusted?

God has presented himself as our heavenly Father and Physician. When Jesus was here, he spent much of his time healing the sick. He had so little time to accomplish his purpose. Why didn't he spend more of it preaching?

It is apparent from all sixty-six books, that God's way is not only to explain but to demonstrate. What was Jesus showing about the Father, and about God's treatment of sinners, by healing all kinds of people the way he did? Some of them never thanked him. Some of them may even have been among his enemies at the end.

Obviously Jesus had not come to picture God as a destroyer. And God will not change in the end. Those who are lost come face to face with a God who is still their Physician, still just as dedicated to helping people live.

Then why does the Bible picture the lost as perishing? They have not been willing to listen. They have not accepted their medicine. They have not followed the Doctor's prescription. What else, then, could the heavenly Physician do but sadly give them up to the consequence?

But why should they go to a doctor they don't trust? Would you trust a doctor who is reputed to be careless with the truth? Would you risk trusting your life to a physician who is said to become angry with his patients and even threaten them with violence?

Ever since the Adversary lied about God in the Garden of

Eden, God has suffered from a forbidding reputation. Even those who present themselves as his friends have often pictured God as arbitrary and severe. The Father understands why so many of his children stay away or go to other healers.

That's why before Jesus went out to Calvary to answer questions about the ultimate consequence of sin, he first lived among us for a while. He wanted us to be assured that the one who finally will have to let some of his children go is an absolutely trustworthy Physician and Friend.

He showed how infinitely loving the Father is by loving everyone, including little children. The disciples assumed that the Savior would be too busy to have time for boys and girls. But Jesus said, "Let the little children come to me, and do not stop them."[5]

He showed how infinitely patient the Father is by treating everyone with utmost courtesy and understanding—even though he was often rebuffed in return. One day the disciples asked if Jesus wanted them to call down fire from heaven to consume the rejecters of his love. The Lord rebuked them for their heartless impatience. He had not come to destroy but to heal.[6]

Jesus wanted us to know that every detail of our lives is of concern to the Father. In all the excitement following the raising of Jairus' daughter, it was Jesus who made sure she had something to eat.[7]

The Supreme Demonstration

Then at the end of his matchless life there came the supreme demonstration of what God is like. On Thursday evening Jesus was arrested. He was illegally tried. He was falsely accused. He was grossly insulted. But not once did he become angry.

Twice he was horribly beaten. All night long he was allowed no sleep, no food. But did he become irritated? Not for a moment.

Men made a game of hitting his wounded head. They jeered at his mysterious birth as illegitimate. They even spat in his face. But did his patience run out? Did he become angry with his tormentors? Never!

Even as they nailed him to the cross, he kept on saying, "Forgive them, Father! They don't know what they are doing."[8]

For Jesus to ask the Father to forgive his tormentors meant that he had already forgiven them himself. None of them had asked for pardon. No one had pleaded with Jesus to forgive them. Jesus forgave them anyway. And remember, Jesus, too, is God.

As Jesus told the disciples, there is no need for him to pray the Father for us, for the Father is just as loving and forgiving as the Son. If the Father had been hanging there instead of Jesus, he would have been just as ready to forgive his tormentors as was the Son—even though no one interceded for them.

What Won the Thief on the Cross?

Two criminals had been crucified with Jesus, one on either side, with Jesus in between. The men were bandits or robbers. The *King James Version* calls them thieves, and many of us have become accustomed to talking about "the thief on the cross."

At first, the two robbers joined in mocking Jesus. Then one of them said to the other, "You know, we deserve to be here, but this man has done nothing wrong." He looked at the inscription posted on Jesus' cross. It read in Hebrew, Latin, and Greek, "This is Jesus, the King of the Jews."

Then Jesus heard words that must for a moment have relieved his pain and made all his suffering seem worth while.

"Jesus, remember me when you come into your kingdom." Jesus agreed that he would.

What was it that won the thief on the cross? Was it hearing Jesus forgive his cruel tormentors? Since the thief had acknowledged he was a criminal, he may well have wondered where he would find himself after he died. A safe place for a man like him would be in a kingdom ruled by such a forgiving king.

"Jesus," the thief may have been thinking, "if *you're* going to have a kingdom, please let me be there."

Then Jesus noticed his mother standing by the cross. Though he was suffering indescribable pain, and though his mind was crowded with thoughts about the meaning of what he was doing, he was concerned about Mary.

John was standing nearby. "Please look after my mother," Jesus asked. From that time on, John kept her in his home.

Soon after this, Jesus died. And as he died, he did not ask, "God, why are you killing me? Why are you executing me?"

No.

Jesus cried, "My God, my God, why have you forsaken me? Why have you given me up? Why have you let me go?"[9]

Though he had never been rebellious for a moment, Jesus was experiencing the final consequence of sin. God was treating him as if he were an unsavable sinner.

"He made him to be sin who knew no sin," was Paul's explanation later.[10] As the *Revised English Bible* puts it, "Christ was innocent of sin, and yet for our sake God made him one with human sinfulness."

I've often heard it said that when sinners die at the end, God will be "pouring out his wrath" upon them.

At the cross, God "poured out his wrath" on his Son. That means, as Paul explains in his letter to Rome, that God "gave him up," "handed him over," "let him go." And in Romans 4:25, Paul states that when Jesus died, he was indeed "given up"—the same Greek word Paul used in Romans 1:24, 26, 28, to explain what happens when God shows his wrath.

Some translations of Romans 4:25 say that Jesus was "put to death." When he was "given up," he did indeed die. One could say that he was "given up" to death. But the Greek only says he was "given up," or "handed over." Paul may have deliberately chosen that Greek word to help us understand what it was that Jesus' death was meant to demonstrate.

The Purpose of the Demonstration

In this memorable passage in his letter to Rome, Paul states the ultimate purpose of Christ's death on the cross:

> God showed him publicly dying as a means of reconciliation to be taken advantage of by faith. This was to demonstrate God's own righteousness, for in his divine forbearance, he had apparently overlooked people's former sins. It was to demonstrate his righteousness at the present time, to show that he himself is righteous and that he sets right everyone who trusts in Jesus.[11]

Paul could not have stated more emphatically that the purpose of the cross was to demonstrate the truth about God's own character, the truth that is the basis of our friendship and trust.

The View from Gethsemane and the Cross

I have often imagined being there the day Jesus was crucified. In fact, I like to imagine going earlier to watch him in the Garden of Gethsemane.

There Jesus begins to experience the separation from the

Father that comes from being "given up" like a sinner. As he feels his unity with the Father breaking up, his agony is almost too much to bear. Mark records that Jesus said, "My soul is overwhelmed with sorrow to the point of death."[12]

Luke the physician reports that an angel from heaven appeared to Jesus and strengthened him. "And being in anguish, he prayed more earnestly, and his sweat was like drops of blood falling to the ground."[13]

Angels, Too, Have Questions

Is God punishing his Son? Is he about to kill him? Angels are watching.[14] They, too, need to see the answer to Satan's charge that the Creator has lied. They were listening in Eden as the Serpent mocked God's warning to Adam and Eve that if they sinned they would die. If God has failed to tell the truth, that is the end of trust. And without trust, there can be no friendship in the family.

Angels have watched as the Adversary has led to a perversion of the meaning of those words of warning. The warning of sin's inevitable consequence has been changed into an arbitrary threat.

Angels have watched the baleful effect of this distortion of the truth. How it has poisoned people's attitude toward God and their practice of religion!

For thousands of years people have offered sacrifice — sometimes even their own children — to win the favor of offended gods. Even in the Christian world, some teach that had it not been for Christ's appeasement of a wrathful God, we would long ago have been destroyed.

Is it true that if the Son were not constantly pleading in our behalf, the Father could not find it in his own heart to forgive and heal his children? In the upper room with his disciples, Jesus plainly and clearly stated his correction of that misunderstanding.[15]

Now angels watch as God the Father and God the Son together demonstrate the truth. What angels witness here in Gethsemane, and later on Calvary, will answer their questions with evidence that will preserve trust and friendship in God's family for eternity.

The angels know who Jesus is. He is their Creator and their God. They watch to see what is happening to the one they love and adore. Is the Father taking away the life of his Son?

The angels listened to Jesus' explanation to his disciples: "No one takes it from me, but I lay it down of my own accord. I have power to lay it down, and I have power to take it up again." [16] Angels know that only God has such power. Now they watch as Jesus falls dying to the ground.

The Questions Are Answered

Is it true that sin results in death?

Yes. Jesus died the death that is "the wages of sin." God had told the truth to Adam and Eve.

Did God kill his Son?

No. He gave him up, as he will give up sinners at the end. It's true that "the wages of sin is death." [17] But God is not the one who imposes those wages. It is sin itself that pays. "Sin pays its servants: the wage is death," is Phillips' translation.

A Third Question

We could ask another question: "Why, God, is it necessary that we understand you are not the executioner? As Sovereign of the universe, you have a perfect right to destroy disobedient servants."

"That's just the point," God might reply. "I don't want to

treat you as servants. I don't want you to stay just servants. I want you to be my friends."

"My children throughout the universe," I can almost hear God say, "I want you to understand that the obedience that springs from fear can produce the character of a rebel. Even as you fearfully obey me, you will be turning against me. Please go to Calvary and see that demonstrated."

There, as in Gethsemane, Jesus experiences separation from the Father. "Why have you forsaken me, why have you let me go?" he cries. Again God does not lay a destroying hand on his Son.

But this time, on Calvary, Jesus is tortured, and in one of the slowest and most cruel ways his enemies have available. If they could have burned him slowly in the fire, they might have chosen that instead.

But who is demanding that Jesus be treated this way?—some of the most obedient servants God has ever had. At least, they certainly appear to be.

They believe in God the Creator, and greatly reverence his authority and power.

They believe in the Bible and read it all the time. Jesus commended them for it.[18]

They accept all ten of the Ten Commandments, and have even added extra rules to help them obey in detail.

They pay more than a double tithe. They eat nothing that is forbidden. And they keep themselves separate from unbelievers, lest they be contaminated.

They may look like obedient servants, but they can hardly be God's friends. At least, they are not the friends of Jesus, and they seem confused as to who he might be. They told him he must be demon-possessed to describe God the way he does.[19]

Now in God's name they demand he be tortured to death.

They must think their heavenly Master will be pleased with such faithful service.

What about the Fire?

Frequently the Bible describes the destruction of the wicked in "eternal fire." Jesus himself spoke of the day when he would have to say to the lost, "Depart from me into the eternal fire prepared for the devil and his angels."[20]

But what is this "eternal fire"? The prophet Isaiah describes people who are not destroyed by "the everlasting flames."

"Who among us can live with the
      devouring fire?
   Who among us can live with
      everlasting flames?"
Those who walk righteously and
      speak uprightly,
   who despise the gain of
      oppression,
who wave away a bribe instead of
      accepting it,
   who stop their ears from
      hearing of bloodshed
   and shut their eyes from looking
      on evil.[21]

The glory that surrounds God is often described in the Bible as having the appearance of fire. When God came down to Mount Sinai, "the appearance of the glory of the Lord was like a devouring fire on the top of the mountain in the sight of the people of Israel."[22]

When Daniel recorded his vision of heaven, he described God's throne as "fiery flames, and its wheels were burning fire. A stream of fire issued and flowed out from his presence." [23]

When Ezekiel described his vision of God, he spoke repeatedly of the appearance of brightness and fire: "This was the appearance of the likeness of the glory of the Lord." [24] When he described the position of the angel Lucifer before his fall, he pictured him in the very presence of God, walking "among the stones of fire." [25]

Even when such a trusted friend as Moses asked to see God in his glory, the Lord replied, "My face you cannot see, for no mortal may see me and live." [26] Yet when Moses came down from talking with God on the mountain, his own face reflected so much of the divine glory that he had to wear a veil out of consideration for the people. [27]

When God said that no mortal could see his face and live, he was not threatening that he would kill anyone he caught peeking. To people, in their present sinful state, the unveiled glory of God would be a consuming fire.

Sin so changes the sinner that it actually results in death. Out of harmony with his Creator, he cannot endure the life-giving glory of his presence.

How, then, could God save sinners? How could he come close enough to win them back to trust? How could he show them that he is a Friend of whom there's no need to be afraid?

God's answer was to send his Son in human form. Though he is himself the "radiance of the glory of God," [28] Jesus "emptied himself, . . . being born in human likeness." [29] He veiled the dazzling splendor of his divinity that human beings might come to know God without being consumed.

Some day God will unveil his glory. He longs to return

this world to normal, as it was in the beginning. In Eden, God could walk and talk with our first parents without any veil between.[30] But ever since sin began to work its deadly changes, God in mercy has veiled his glory. As Peter explains, our heavenly Father is very patient with us, "not wanting anyone to perish, but everyone to come to repentance."[31]

Repentance means changing our minds. Graciously God continues to grant us time and opportunity to consider the evidence. If we decide he can be trusted, and then go on trusting him enough to stay with him and let him heal the damage sin has done, the time will come when once again we can live in that glory.

Moses and Elijah were healed, or they could never have stood with Christ on the Mount of Transfiguration. On that memorable day, two former sinners stood in the unveiled glory of God.

But when God unveils his glory in the end, all that is out of harmony will be consumed. On that awesome day, the saved and the lost alike will all be standing in the "devouring fire," "the everlasting flames," of God's glory.

Why are the lost the only ones consumed? There is nothing arbitrary about this. It has nothing to do with legal standing. God doesn't finally give the order, "Burn these, keep those!" The difference is simply in *us*.

As God watches untold numbers of his rebellious children die, he will be crying, as in the book of Hosea, "How can I give you up! How can I let you go!"

While God is weeping over the loss of his children, I can't imagine that any of the saved would be engaged in joyful celebration, as I've heard some suggest that they will. I see them gathering around the Father, as Peter, James and John could have done as Jesus suffered in Gethsemane. Perhaps John, the one who watched Jesus die, might even venture to say, "Don't cry, God. There's nothing more you could have done."

The Price of Answering the Questions

Think what it cost the Father, the Son, and the Spirit of Truth, to answer these essential questions — not just to state the answers, but to demonstrate the truth.

The demonstration was so painful that surely only someone who is our best Friend would be willing to show us. But since the only one who could answer these questions is God himself, only our best Friend *could* show us.

The Power of the Cross to Win Friends

Near the beginning of this book I told of the Shakespearean actress who stood outside the theatre in the Bard's old home town and explained her rejection of God. You may recall that she said, "The gods of other religions are less cruel than the God of the Old Testament!"

A young actor was standing beside her. He did not argue with what she had said, because he could understand what had led her to that position. But he did say that he believed in God himself. In fact, he said he was a Christian.

"How did you become a believer?" I inquired.

"Well, I haven't been one all my life," he replied. "It happened only recently. Someone gave me a copy of the Gospel of John."

"What did you read there that made you want to be a Christian?"

"The story of the cross," he answered without hesitation.

"What was it about the cross?" I asked, wondering what theory of the atonement he might have heard.

"It was the way Jesus behaved on the cross," he went on very thoughtfully. "To think that such a good person would be hanging there. Jesus had never done anything wrong, or hurt anybody. Yet they were torturing him to death.

"And while they were hurting him," he continued, "Jesus was saying that he forgave them. Then he said that the Father was just like him. There was something about Jesus that made me want to believe that. And if God is just like Jesus, I surely would trust him.

"That's what made me want to be a Christian."

here are many free-doms that come with the kind of friendship Jesus described in John 15:15.

There is freedom from the tyranny of the arbitrary ex-ercise of authority. We may ask questions. God wants us to understand.

There is freedom to speak plainly and clearly, as Job and David did. When the Psalmist talked to God, he was very can-did about the subject being discussed. If he hated someone, he did not try to hide it in dark speech. If he wanted vengeance on his enemies, he asked plainly for their destruction.

"O that you would kill the wicked, O God," he prayed in Psalm 139. Then afterwards he added,

> Search me, O God, and know my heart;
> > test me and know my thoughts.
> See if there is any wicked way in me,
> > and lead me in the way everlasting. (NRSV)

David knew that God wanted him to be especially honest in their relationship with each other. David had not always been this way. So he prayed in Psalm 51:

"I don't condemn you either."

You desire truth in the inward being;
therefore teach me wisdom in
my secret heart. . . .
Create in me a clean heart,
O God,
and put a new and right spirit
within me. (NRSV)

Freedom from Fear

To be one of God's understanding friends means to be free from fear of God himself. Obviously, there is no need to be afraid of a God who wants us to be his friends. And he never has threatened, "Be my friend or I'll destroy you."

Even when facing the judgment, we have no need to fear. This is not because we have a friend between us and our holy God. God himself is our friend.

This freedom from fear may be tested for a brief moment when we come face to face with God in the hereafter. How do you expect to feel when you come that close to God? Moses was so overwhelmed with awe when God came down on Sinai that he said, "I tremble with fear."[1] But soon he was able to reassure the people that there was no need to be afraid.

Will this freedom from fear last for eternity? What will it be like to live in the presence of a God who knows all about us — everything! Will he haunt us with the memory of our sinful past?

How Jesus Treated the Adulterous Woman and Her Accusers

For an answer we have only to watch how Jesus treated all kinds of sinners. One of the most dramatic examples can be found in the story of the woman caught in adultery. As translated in the *New International Version*, the story reads like this:

> At dawn he [Jesus] appeared again in the temple courts, where all the people gathered around him, and he sat down to teach them. The teachers of the law and the Pharisees brought in a woman caught in adultery. They made her stand before the group and said to Jesus, "Teacher, this woman was caught in the act of adultery. In the Law Moses commanded us to stone such women. Now what do you say?" They were using this question as a trap, in order to have a basis for accusing him.
>
> But Jesus bent down and started to write on the ground with his finger. When they kept on questioning him, he straightened up and said to them, "If any one of you is without sin, let him be the first to throw a stone at her." Again he stooped down and wrote on the ground.
>
> At this, those who heard began to go away one at a time, the older ones first, until only Jesus was left, with the woman still standing there. Jesus straightened up and asked her, "Woman, where are they? Has no one condemned you?"
>
> "No one, sir," she said.
>
> "Then neither do I condemn you," Jesus declared. "Go now and leave your life of sin." [2]

Evidently the early Christians did not know what to do with this story, for it appears in different places in the manuscripts, or sometimes not at all. Your version may have a note of explanation. But many scholars are of the opinion that the story does belong in the Bible. It is hardly the kind of story that would have been made up in Jesus' day or created by the typical manuscript copyist in later years.

The distinguished Princeton scholar Bruce Metzger, in his book *The Text of the New Testament*, agrees that "the story... has all the earmarks of historical veracity; no ascetically minded monk would have invented a narrative which closes with what seems to be only a mild rebuke on Jesus' part."

Some religious leaders brought this poor woman to Christ in another attempt to trap him into contradicting the teachings of the Old Testament. Each attempt to entrap him Jesus met with his customary skill and grace.

This time, to make sure that they could carry the crowds with them, the enemies of Christ made certain that they had the necessary evidence. In the hearing of the whole onlooking crowd they announced that "this woman was caught in the very act."

Then they posed their question: "You know the teaching of the Old Testament on this matter. You know the rule about what ought to be done with a woman like this. Will you agree that she ought to be stoned?" The public watched to see what Jesus would say.

He said nothing. He just bent down and began to write with his finger in the dust. A puff of wind, a few footsteps, and the record would be gone. Then his conscience-pricking words: "If any of you is without sin, let him be the first to throw a stone at her."

Why didn't Jesus draw the whole crowd closer and say, "Let me tell you a few things about these accusers of this poor woman." Didn't they deserve to be exposed? What does it say about God that his Son did not publicly humiliate those self-righteous men?

This is what Christ came to reveal. God finds no pleasure in our embarrassment, in exposing our sins to others.

When they had all gone, Jesus turned to the woman and gently said, "I don't condemn you either. Go home, and don't sin again." Graciously he tried to restore the dishonored woman's self-respect.

How Jesus Treated Simon

Simon, a wealthy man whom Jesus had cured of leprosy, invited Jesus and other friends to eat with him at his house. Three of Jesus' closest friends were also there: Lazarus and his sisters, Martha and Mary. Mary is described by Luke as "a woman who was living an immoral life in the town."[3]

While they were all reclining at the table, Mary brought a flask of very costly perfume and anointed Jesus' feet and wiped them with her hair. Simon watched with disapproval and thought to himself, "'If this man were a prophet, he would know who is touching him and what kind of woman she is — that she is a sinner.'

"Jesus answered him, 'Simon, I have something to tell you.'"

"'Tell me, teacher,' he said."[4]

Jesus then told a story of two debtors who both had been forgiven. And as he told it, Simon realized that Jesus had read his thoughts. He began to see himself as a worse sinner than the woman he had despised, and he wondered if Jesus might go on and expose him before his guests.

Nothing is more offensive to the Lord than self-righteous accusation. But did he expose Simon? Did he say to the company, "Let me tell you about our host"?

Instead, the Lord as always did the gracious thing. He courteously accepted Mary's impulsive act. With equal grace he corrected Simon without humiliating him before his friends. Simon must have been deeply touched!

The Paralytic at the Pool of Bethesda

When Jesus met the paralytic at the Pool of Bethesda, he did not humiliate or condemn him for having squandered his health in youthful indulgence. He simply asked him kindly, "Would you like to be well? Then pick up your mat and go home." Later Jesus met him and said, "You know what caused your trouble. Go and sin no more, lest something worse happen to you."[5]

The Misbehaving Disciples

Picture Jesus in the upper room the night before he was crucified. The twelve disciples were squabbling like children as to "which one of them was to be regarded as the greatest."[6]

Did Jesus chide them for their folly or scold them for their unwillingness to wash each other's feet? Instead, he quietly arose, took a towel and a basin of water, and the universe watched as the great Creator knelt down and washed a dozen pairs of dirty feet. He even washed the feet of his betrayer, Judas.

What a chance the disciples missed to wash the feet of the Son of God the night before he died! If only one of them had volunteered, "Please, Lord, may I wash your feet?" What a memory he would have cherished for the rest of eternity!

But instead, Jesus was the only one in the room that night who ate his supper with dirty feet. I wonder how onlooking angels felt.

Imagine the effect on the disciples as each in turn looked down on the head of Jesus bent over the basin and felt those strong carpenter's hands washing his feet.

Jesus could have looked up at them and said, "You don't believe my Father would be willing to do this, do you? But if you have seen me, you have seen the Father. The Father loves you just as much as I do. If you are comfortable with me, you will be comfortable with him."

Judas

Later Jesus said that one of them would betray him. But he didn't expose him to the whole group. When he told Judas to go and do quickly the terrible thing he had to do, the other disciples thought he had been sent out for provisions or even to perform such a noble act as to give an offering to the poor.

Why didn't Jesus expose his betrayer before the others? Surely he deserved to be exposed. Think what it says about God that Jesus did not humiliate such a traitor!

Peter, James, and John

Later that night, out in Gethsemane, Jesus took Peter, James, and John still deeper into the Garden and there began his awesome experience of separation from his Father. Three times he came over to where the disciples were dozing, hoping for some companionship and comfort in his agony.

What a chance the disciples missed to encourage the Son of God! What if the three of them had arisen and gone back with Jesus and knelt down around him as he prayed? Isn't that what real friends would do? What a memory those three men would have had! But they slept through it all. And Jesus did not reprove them. He sympathized with them for being too tired to help.

Peter

A few hours later Peter was cursing and swearing in the courtyard to prove he was not one of Christ's disciples. He did not even know him!

Then the rooster crowed, just as Jesus had predicted the night before—right after Peter's bold speech that, though others might let him down, he would give his life for the Lord.

When Peter heard that sound, he looked to see if Jesus had noticed. Though he was on trial for his life and had suffered so much already, Jesus was more concerned about his erring disciple out there in the courtyard. He turned and looked straight at Peter.

As Peter knew God up to that time, he may well have expected to see wrath and indignation in the face of Christ. He surely deserved it! But instead he saw sorrow, disappointment, and pity—the face of the one who just the night before had knelt down and washed his dirty feet.

Peter went out and wept bitterly.[7]

A little later Judas came into the court, threw down the thirty pieces of silver, and confessed that he had betrayed innocent blood. Then he, too, looked at Jesus. He saw the same sorrow and pity that had touched Peter's heart — the face of the one who just the night before had knelt down and washed his dirty feet. Overcome, Judas went out and hanged himself.[8]

If only Judas had responded as Peter did to that look on Jesus' face! If Judas had found where Peter was weeping and the two disciples had knelt down together and become new men, what a scene that would have been for all heaven to watch.

Imagine how Peter felt all that Sabbath. What a fool he had made of himself the past twenty-four hours! Twice he had spoken impetuously in the upper room. Twice he had disgraced himself in the Garden of Gethsemane. And such cowardice and disloyalty while his Lord was being tried! Now Jesus was dead, and there was no chance for him to make things right.

No wonder he rushed to the tomb on Sunday morning when he heard the news that the grave was empty!

Mary

But it was Mary who had the privilege of seeing Christ first and carrying the good news to the other disciples — Mary, of all people, the woman who had so many problems and so many weaknesses![9] Yet it was Mary who was picked for this high privilege. Think what it says about God that Mary should be the one so highly honored.

When Mary recognized Jesus standing outside the tomb, she fell at his feet to worship him. And Jesus gently said, "Do not detain me now, for I have not yet ascended to my Father. But go and tell my brothers that I am going up to my Father and your Father, to my God and your God."[10]

Listen to Jesus calling the disciples his brothers — the men who had let him down when he needed them the most!

When the angels confirmed Jesus' command to Mary to take the news to the disciples, they said, "Tell the disciples, and especially tell Peter, that Jesus has risen and will meet them in Galilee."[11]

How godlike of the angels to add, "and especially tell Peter"! The angels admire and worship God for the way he has treated sinners. How they must have enjoyed adding, "Tell Peter"!

This is the kind of God with whom we may spend eternity. That's why, even though we all have sinned, we'll be comfortable in the presence of the one who knows us so well.

We have nothing to fear from the infinite memory of God. There's no limit to his willingness to forgive. And he has promised not only to forgive us but to treat us as if we had never sinned. He will cast all our sins behind his back.[12] He will "send them to the bottom of the sea!"[13]

There is no pretense or forgetfulness in this. God knows how we have lived. We know what sinners we have been. Angels have watched our every deed. But in spite of all this, our heavenly Father will treat us with dignity and respect as if we had always been his loyal children.

Is this only a promise, or has God actually demonstrated his willingness to treat former sinners like this? After King David died, God talked to David's son Solomon about his famous father.

And God said, "If you will walk in my ways, keeping my statutes and my commandments, as your father David walked, then I will lengthen your life."[14] But David had committed some notorious sins. How could God describe him as keeping all his commandments?

Something had happened to David since those transgressions. He had come to realize that God wanted truth in the inner man. So he had asked God to search his heart and purify that place where a man does his thinking. In response to his prayer, God had given him a new heart and a right spirit. Now once again God could speak of David as "a man after my own heart."[15]

Evidently God really means it when he says he will put our sins behind his back. In the hereafter, if we are admitted to his kingdom, God will even speak of us to others as if we had always been his loyal friends. And to make sure we are comfortable, God will not admit a single gossip there![16]

Would We Be More Comfortable with the Son?

Who would you rather meet first when you arrive in the kingdom — the Father, or the Son? I have asked that question of hundreds of people. Most have responded that probably it would be the Son.

What if you *do* meet Jesus first? A little later, he asks if you are ready now to go and see the Father.

Would you say, "Yes, if you'll go with me"?

Now you're standing with Jesus in the awesome presence of the Father. Your head is bowed, and you're staring at the floor.

You hear a warm and resonant voice say, "You can look at me, if you want to."

You look up and see a face just as kind as the face of the Son. You begin to apologize, "Oh I'm sorry, God, that I was scared. Jesus *said* that if we have seen him, we have seen you. He *told* us that you love us as much as he does, and that you want us to be your friends."

"That's all right," says the same warm, resonant voice. "Now you know the truth. *Now* can we be friends?"

"I'm Not Afraid to Die"

Several years ago I buried an old friend and former student. He had been an officer in the air force and had led more than 50 bombing raids over Europe during the Second World War. When the war was over, he turned up in one of my classes in New Testament Greek, preparing himself to be a minister. He was an outstanding student. Frequently we talked together about our picture of God.

For the next 35 years, he served as a dearly-loved pastor. Now he was dying of cancer. As I stood by his bed in the hospital, he reached out his hand and spoke quietly:

"You know, Graham, I'm not afraid to die. And you know the reason why. We share the same picture of God."

FRIENDSHIP AND THE STRUGGLE WITH SIN

aul reassured the believers in Rome that since we have been "justified by faith, we have peace with God through our Lord Jesus Christ."[1]

Your favorite version of the Bible may not say "we have peace" but rather "let us have peace." The difference lies in the spelling of the Greek word for "have." Since the manuscripts are quite divided between the two spellings, the decision must be based on one's understanding of the whole passage. New Testament scholars have debated the matter for many years, sometimes with considerable heat!

In the meantime, Moffatt's 1913 translation still offers a good bridge between the two choices: "Let us enjoy the peace we have."

The Meaning of Justification

It is a law that we become like the person we worship and admire.

The more important question in this verse is, What does it mean to be "justified"? Your version may not use this word at all. For some, this Latin-based English term is simply more "dark speech."

The Greek word Paul used means basically to set something right. The *Good News Bible* translates this verse, "Now that we have been put right with God through faith, we have peace with God."

Servant-believers understand that what needs to be put right between them and their offended Master is primarily a legal matter. The solution to this problem, as they see it, is forgiveness and the adjustment of their legal standing. They use the word "justification" to mean pardon and the declaration that now they are legally right with God. This brings peace with God, they say, because now they need have no fear of his wrath, or of punishment, or of loss of reward.

But pardon alone doesn't bring real peace. Have you ever been forgiven for something disgraceful and then, because of the embarrassment, found yourself avoiding the one who had been so forgiving? After we've been "justified by faith," God doesn't want us to avoid him in embarrassment. He wants us to be close friends.

Friend-believers have a different understanding of justification — if one must use that word at all. What has gone wrong, they believe, is primarily a breach of faith, a break-down of trust and trustworthiness. To set this right, trust must be restored. To be right with God means to trust him and to be his trustworthy friend. This, of course, means peace. Paul puts trust, peace, and being right with God, all together in this verse. That makes very good sense to friends.

Why Then the Struggle?

The apostle Paul had long enjoyed peace with God. But he was far from being at peace with himself. He admitted this to the Roman believers:

"Oh, the good that I want to do, I don't do. And the evil that I don't want to do, is what I go on doing. Wretched man that I am, who will deliver me from this doomed body?"2

Paul tries to explain his conflict. "I have the desire to do what is good, but I cannot carry it out. . . .

"So I find this law at work: When I want to do good, evil is right there with me. For in my inner being I delight in God's law; but I see another law at work in the members of my body, waging war against the law of my mind and making me a prisoner of the law of sin at work within my members."3

"A man who talks like that must not be converted," some have said. But many devout believers have discovered from their own experience that Paul's struggle can continue for the rest of one's life. Of course, no matter when the struggle is felt, the solution remains the same: "Thanks be to God — through Jesus Christ our Lord!"4

The Greek word for "wretched" can include the meaning of "worn out by hard work." Paul sounds like a saint who is really trying — but weary from the continued effort.

It seems to me that Paul is describing the transition from struggling as a mere servant and struggling as an understanding friend.

Even before he became a Christian, he had been absolutely committed to obeying all ten of the Ten Commandments. He mentioned to the believers at Philippi that in his practice of the law, he was a "Pharisee," which meant that he was scrupulously obedient. "By the law's standard of righteousness," Paul continued, he was "without fault."5

He had not been a thief. He had not committed adultery. He had not murdered anyone. According to his understanding at that time, what he did to Stephen wasn't murder. It was only doing the work of the Lord in stamping out heresy. More than that, he had always paid a faithful tithe. In fact, he had kept every single rule that he was aware of.

But after Paul met Jesus on the Damascus road, he began to take a closer look at the Commandments. He heard that Jesus had taught that mere external conformity to those rules was not what God wanted. That's the kind of obedience you get from a servant. God hopes we will see that there is nothing arbitrary about the Commandments. They describe the behavior of loving, friendly, trustworthy people, who not only don't murder — they don't hate. They not only don't commit adultery — they don't even want to.

Paul must have recognized that Moses had taught this long before. When Moses said that the Israelites should love their neighbors as themselves, he added, "You shall not hate in your heart...or bear a grudge."[6]

Paul's attention was drawn especially to the tenth commandment.[7] In the light of what Moses and Jesus had taught, he realized that "You shall not covet" includes not even *wanting* to do something that is wrong.

As the meaning of that commandment dawned on Paul, it made him angry, he confessed. He had tried so hard. At times he had even wanted to break one of the Ten, but he had successfully resisted the temptation. Didn't he deserve credit for not giving in? And shouldn't he get extra credit, he may have thought, for being still in the prime of life and resisting stronger urges than other people?

I once had a college teacher who was incredibly energetic. He was also an inspiring Christian gentleman. But he was plagued with an explosive temper, which sometimes got out of control.

"You must remember," he explained to some of us students one day, "I have probably resisted more temptation to lose my temper than any of you have ever felt!" He made me think of Paul.

But later, Paul's irritation at the command not to covet turned into agreement and admiration. To obey number ten would be the key to obeying all the others. To come to the place where he didn't even want to sin would mean receiving what David had asked for, a new heart and a right spirit.

No longer was Paul concerned about credit. Why should he be rewarded for doing something that was so beneficial to himself? And as far as the constant conflict was concerned, God assured him that he wasn't condemned for struggling.[8]

Doctors Don't Condemn Their Patients

Doctors don't condemn their struggling patients. They know healing takes time. They don't expect an injured patient to sprint home from the first office visit.

God works like an infinitely skillful physician. He can save and heal anyone who trusts him. He is not at all satisfied when we come to his office just to be forgiven. He proposes to bring us to the place where we won't have to ask for forgiveness any more. He offers to heal that place where people do their thinking. Then they won't violate those rules any more, because they don't even want to, and all the bad habits are gone.

To some, that sounds ominously like perfection. And to many servant-believers, that is the ultimately burdensome requirement. "You are to be perfect" is Goodspeed's brilliant translation of Matthew 5:48. Servants see those words as a command. Friends see them as a promise.

Friends don't want God to settle for anything less. Would

you ask a physician not to heal you completely? Would you say, "Seventy-five per cent healing will be quite sufficient, thank you"?

Requirement or Generous Offer?

To servants, who think of salvation as dealing with their legal problems, perfection is yet another requirement. To friends, who think of salvation as healing the damage sin has done, perfection is an incredibly generous offer.

Servants want to be completely forgiven. Friends want to be completely healed.

Jesus didn't come just to forgive sin. He came to do away with it. As Paul explains, God sent his son "to deal with sin," (NRSV)[9] "to do away with sin." (GNB)[10]

Forgiveness does not do away with sin. Sin is not something recorded in a book, to be forgiven from time to time. Sin is something that happens in people. Sin is rebellion and distrust. This is what Jesus came to eliminate. And the antidote for such sin is the truth about God himself.

"About that matter of perfection," the heavenly Physician might call after us, as we walk away from his office. "Don't worry about that at all. I've so designed my universe that it's a law people become like the person they worship and admire.

"If you really stay my trusting friends, perfection will come. I'm not saying you won't struggle any more. But the struggle won't be the same."

Servants struggle to overcome sin by trying to stamp it out. Friends know they can only get rid of sin by crowding it out with the truth.

12   FRIENDSHIP AND THE
MEANING OF ATONEMENT

ecently I received an invitation to attend a religious convention where much of the time would be spent discussing the Christian teaching about atonement.

If one of these invitations had been sent to the apostle Paul, he would have been puzzled about the subject chosen.

"What is this word 'atonement?' " he might have inquired.

"Don't you remember, Paul? It's that special word you gave us in your letter to Rome."

"I don't recall using it at all."

"Oh, we're not suggesting you used the English word. We mean the Greek word that we English-speaking people translate into the word 'atonement.' "

"Well," Paul ponders, "perhaps it would help me remember if you could tell me where in Romans I'm supposed to have used this word."

"It's about a third of the way through your letter, Paul. We've invented chapters and verses since you died, and it makes

"You mean I can come home?"

159

it much easier to find your place. We call the passage Romans 5:10, 11."

Paul finds the place and begins to read — thoughtfully translating it all into English!

"We were God's enemies," Paul begins, sounding very much like the translation of the *Good News Bible*, "but he made us his friends through the death of his Son. Now that we are God's friends, how much more will we be saved by Christ's life! But that is not all; we rejoice because of what God has done through our Lord Jesus Christ, who has now made us God's friends."[1]

"That's the place right there," you interrupt. "There at the end, where you said 'who has now made us God's friends.' That's where you used the Greek word for atonement."

"No, that's the regular word for 'reconciliation,'" Paul corrects. "And I simply warmed up that word 'reconciliation' a bit by translating it 'making friends.'"

"But," Paul continues, "if the English word 'atonement' really means 'reconciliation,' 'making friends,' I could correctly use the word 'atonement' next time I translate this passage in Romans. But tell me, my English-speaking friend, what do *you* mean by the word 'atonement'?"

What Does the Word "Atonement" Mean?

If the *King James Version* had not chosen to use the word "atonement" in the last line of Romans 5:11, we might not be raising this question. Actually, this is the only occurrence of the word "atonement" in the entire New Testament of the *King James Version*. And in the margin of this verse, later editors of the *King James* have added a note reminding the reader that this is the regular word for "reconciliation."

If you really want to find the meaning of an English word, settle for nothing less than the multivolume *Oxford English Dic-*

tionary. In that enormous lexicon you can trace the historical development of the meaning of a word.

Volume One explains that the term "atonement" was made up of "at" and "one" and "ment." At-one-ment.

That great old dictionary shows how back in the thirteenth century the word "atonement" was used to mean "being at one," "being in harmony," the opposite of "being at odds." And the verb "to atone" meant in those days "to set at one," "to unite." There was even a verb back then that was pronounced "to one." Not w-o-n, but o-n-e. Peacemakers still try to "one" enemies.

A Later Change in the Meaning

Dictionaries all seem to agree that the original meaning of atonement was "harmony, concord, agreement, unity of feeling." And the verb "to atone" used to mean "to restore friendly relations between persons who have been at variance; hence, reconciliation."

These early meanings, however, are now marked as "archaic and obsolete." In 1611, when the *King James* committee decided to use the word "atonement" in Romans 5:11, they understood it in that old, "archaic" sense.

As time passed, the word "atonement" came to be used more and more to denote "appeasement, making amends, paying a penalty to satisfy legal demands." As the *Oxford English Dictionary* observes, "Here the idea of reconciliation or reunion is practically lost sight of under that of legal satisfaction or amends."

In common speech today, we often use the word "atone" in this later sense of making amends.

A husband comes home much too late to take his wife out to dinner as he had promised — on their wedding anniversary, no less! On the way home he desperately picks up a box of her favorite chocolates and a large bunch of beautiful roses. These he presents repentantly at the door. (In theology, that's called appeasement or propitiation).

After considerable effort, at least some measure of communication is re-established between husband and wife. The wife comes up with a solution.

"Husband," she announces, "you can atone for this disgraceful thing you've done by taking me out to dinner every Monday night for the rest of the year." Now, that's atonement in the later sense of the word.

Hopefully those efforts to make amends will result in reconciliation and at-one-ment between that husband and wife. The unity of such at-one-ment is the original meaning of the word "atonement."

What Jesus Said about Atonement

When someone asks what I think atonement means, I sometimes reply, when the circumstances are appropriate, "I like what Jesus said about it."

"But Jesus never talked about atonement, did he?"

I'll agree that Jesus never used the word — nor did anyone else in Scripture, including Paul. But I believe Jesus had a good deal to say about atonement. That is, if you understand atonement in the old, "archaic" sense of reconciliation and making friends. Look, for example, at what he said to his Father in that memorable prayer recorded in John 17.

"I ask not only on behalf of these," Jesus prayed, referring to his disciples, "but also on behalf of those who will believe in me through their word, that they may all be one."[2] Now, *that's* at-one-ment. "As you, Father, are in me and I am in you, may they also be in us," Jesus continued praying.

What does it mean to be "in somebody"? If Jesus is in me, and I am in him, and he is in the Father, and the Father is in him — I want to know who is in whom, or if anybody is really *in* anyone else.

This being "in" another person has been understood by many to mean "in union with," and it is often so translated. The union God desires with his friends is so close that it's like being "in" each other. Though we're individual persons, we can be in such close union with each other that it's as if we were one.

The relationship between the Father and the Son is presented in the Bible as the ultimate model of at-one-ment. "The glory that you have given me I have given them," Jesus prayed to his Father, "so that they may be one, as we are one."[3]

The Price of Atonement

Several times Jesus explained what it would cost to restore his universe, his family, to at-one-ment. He used the term that sometimes is translated "ransom," or "redemption price."[4] Then he told what that price would be.

" 'When I am lifted up from the earth, I will draw everyone to me.' (In saying this he indicated the kind of death he was going to suffer.)"[5]

"I will draw *everyone* to me," Jesus said. Not only human beings but angels too are drawn closer into at-one-ment with God as they consider the meaning of the cross.

Paul was in agreement with this understanding. He spoke of God's plan "that the universe, everything in heaven and on earth, might be brought into a unity in Christ."[6]

In another letter, Paul explained that "God was pleased to reconcile to himself all things, whether on earth or in heaven, by making peace through the blood of his cross."[7]

Peace in the Universe

In what sense does the universe need Christ's peace-making sacrifice? Has there ever been a threat to unity, a breach of at-one-ment, in God's heavenly family?

For those of us who are able to take seriously the last of the sixty-six books, Revelation 12 seems to describe a war that began up in heaven. From Genesis to Revelation one can read of the causes and consequences of that war, and why it cost the sufferings and death of Christ to win that war and establish peace for the rest of eternity.

There once was at-one-ment in God's family, before that war began. Back in those days, all of God's children trusted each other. All of them trusted their heavenly Father, and he in turn could safely trust in them. And where there is such mutual trust and trustworthiness, there is peace, harmony, and at-one-ment.

What Went Wrong?

Sadly a conflict of distrust arose, even to the point of open rebellion and war. Disunity and disharmony took the place of unity and at-one-ment. That's how sin entered the universe. As John explains, sin is lawlessness and rebellion.[8] Or, as Paul describes, sin is a breakdown of faith and trust.[9]

The purpose of the plan of salvation is to restore that trust, to bring the rebellion to an end, and thus to establish at-one-ment once again in the whole universe. All of God's children are unavoidably involved.

Some seem to find it disappointing, even offensive, to learn that Christ did not die primarily for them. But unless God wins this war and reestablishes peace in his family, our salvation is meaningless. Who would want to live for eternity in a warring universe?

Without this larger understanding of a conflict that has involved the universe, it's hard to understand Paul's explanation that Jesus shed his blood to bring peace, reconciliation, and unity to God's children in heaven as well as on earth. But recognition of the war and its issues helps one to take a larger view of the cross and of the plan of salvation and atonement.

The kind of unity God desires cannot be commanded or produced by force or fear. In the course of human history, many tyrants have tried to maintain unity by terror and brutality. But that kind of at-one-ment does not last. Look at what has happened in a number of countries just in recent years.

The kind of at-one-ment God desires is described in the New Testament as a unity that is "inherent in our faith and in our knowledge of the Son of God."[10] People who love and trust the same Jesus and the same God are naturally attracted to each other. The same truth about God that sets them free from tyranny and fear binds them together in the firmest kind of unity. Friends of a friendly God enjoy at-one-ment with each other.

This is where the meaning of the cross is so important. There can be no friendship and at-one-ment where there is fear. Calvary says there is no need to be afraid of God. When God says, "Be my friend," he's not saying, "Be my friend or I'll punish you severely; I'll even put you to death." You don't talk that way to friends — especially if you want to keep their friendship. And friendship is the whole purpose and meaning of atonement.

Atonement Means Making Friends

Paul sums this up in a wonderful message he sent to the believers in Corinth. It adds significance to this passage to realize that Paul had just passed through a long and painful period of hostility and distrust with the members of the Corinthian church. But his efforts at reconciliation had finally met with success. In the glow of restored at-one-ment, Paul wrote them these words:

> When anyone is joined to Christ, he is a new being; the old is gone, the new has come. All this is done by God, who through Christ changed us from enemies into his friends and gave us the task of making others his friends also. Our message is that God was making all mankind his friends through Christ. God did not keep an account of their sins, and he has given us the message which tells how he makes them his friends.
>
> Here we are, then, speaking for Christ, as though God himself were making his appeal through us. We plead on Christ's behalf: let God change you from enemies into his friends.[11]

In this passage, the word that is translated "making friends," or "changing into friends," is the Greek word often translated "reconciliation"—and in that one place in the *King James Version* is translated "atonement."

It seems to me that the one who made that incredible offer of friendship in John 15:15 must love this American Bible Society translation of Paul's jubilant message to the believers in Corinth.

"You Mean I Can Come Home?"

One of the Lord's most memorable parables was about atonement—in the original sense of that word. Jesus told about a son who wasted his life and his share of his father's estate in riotous self-indulgence. Now penniless and starving, he found employment looking after swine.

As he languished there in the pigsty, he began to remember how good it had been at home and wondered if there might be any way to persuade his offended father to let him come back.

His thoughts might have been very different had he known that his father had long been looking down the road, hoping to catch a glimpse of his son coming home. Unfortunately, the son didn't know his father very well.

He began to think of ways to persuade his father to let him in when he arrived at the door. His father could well be very angry with him. Perhaps he should look for his mother first, and she could help persuade his father to forgive and let him have another chance.

And then there was all that money he'd wasted. He would have to find some way to make amends.

"I know what I'll do," the son decided. "I'll ask him to treat me as one of his hired servants." With that, he started out on his way home, practicing his speech as he went.

Had he looked up, he might have noticed his father still watching for him down that road. "But while he was still a long way off his father saw him, and his heart went out to him; he ran to meet him, flung his arms round him, and kissed him.

"The son said, 'Father, I have sinned against God and against you; I am no longer fit to be called your son.'

"But the father said to his servants, 'Quick! Fetch a robe, the best we have, and put it on him . . . and let us celebrate with a feast. For this son of mine was dead and has come back to life; he was lost and is found.'"[12]

At last the son had learned the truth about his father. He didn't even have to finish that speech. His father had forgiven him long before. But he had to come home to find that out. Now his father's forgiveness led him to real repentance.

As the prodigal stood there in his father's arms, he began to experience the original meaning of atonement.

Servants understand atonement as making amends.

Friends understand atonement as making friends.

Now that's atonement!

The Older Brother Was Just a Servant

As the sounds of celebration reached the ears of the older brother, he protested that justice had not been done.

" 'Look,'" he complained to his father, "'all these years I have worked for you like a slave, and I have never disobeyed your orders. What have you given me? Not even a goat for me to have a feast with my friends! But this son of yours wasted all your property on prostitutes, and when he comes back home, you kill the prize calf for him!'"

" 'My son,' the father answered, 'you are always here with me, and everything I have is yours. But we had to celebrate and be happy, because your brother was dead, but now he is alive; he was lost, but now he has been found.'"[13]

In his preoccupation with justice, the older brother refused to attend the party.

The parable doesn't tell if he ever changed his mind.

Dear God,
thank-you for making me,
and for
so we
can
you
P.S.
Leilani

13   WE'VE CAMPED AROUND
THIS MOUNTAIN LONG ENOUGH

ount Sinai is most famous for God's presentation of the law of Ten Commandments, along with many other rules and regulations that he knew the people needed. After they had been thoroughly instructed, he told them it was time to move on. "You have stayed long enough at this mountain," God said. "Break camp and advance."[1]

The Children of Israel had needed that stop at the mountain. They had needed all those added rules and regulations, even all the "dark speech" of ritual and ceremony. They had needed the thunder and lightning, just as much as they had needed the miracles of water and "angels' food." And the God who took them to Sinai was the one who explained later in the upper room, "I'd rather you be my friends."

When Israel finally entered Canaan, they took with them the tablets of the Ten Commandments. If only they had lived up to all those rules of love, the Promised Land would have been an unbelievably safe and pleasant place to live.

But it wasn't long before many began to ignore the Commandments. In those days, the Old Testament records, "Everyone

"Thank you for all 66."

did whatever he pleased."[2] Some of the things they did make rather lurid reading in the book of Judges.

Many forgot the one who had rescued them from Egyptian bondage and had promised them such a golden future in the land that "flowed with milk and honey."[3] Even some of the leaders returned to worshipping idols again.

In the middle of the Ten Commandments, God had included a regulation designed to keep Israel from forgetting him, and to help them remember the good things he had in mind for his people. It was the law of the weekly Sabbath.

Unfortunately, servants were inclined to view that law as a particularly burdensome requirement. "Thou shalt not do anything enjoyable on the Sabbath day," was the way some seemed to read it.

Even today, some servants describe the restful provisions of the Sabbath as arbitrary requirements, meant just to show God's authority and test our willingness to obey.

But Jesus came to show there is no arbitrariness in God. As Paul explained, God's laws were added to help us, to protect us in our ignorance and immaturity, and to lead us back to trust. This must also be true of the weekly Sabbath.

Fortunately, God's friends have helped explain his purpose in giving this regulation. Isaiah even says that if you don't enjoy the Sabbath, you're not really observing it anyway![4]

Obviously, then, Sabbath observance cannot be commanded or enforced. "Enjoy the Sabbath, or you'll be severely punished!" Such a command would make no sense at all. If your child is not very fond of spinach, would you order her to tell you how delicious it is, or she'll be severely punished?

But what could be so enjoyable about observing the weekly Sabbath? It helps to read the rest of the Bible to find very significant reasons.

Servants, who simply do what they're told, tend to see the Sabbath as a limitation of their freedom—a restriction that faithful servants are quite willing to accept.

Friends understand the Sabbath as a monument to friendship, a reminder of the evidence that is the basis for freedom and trust.

Some Prefer to Linger at Sinai

Servant-believers tend to linger indefinitely at Mount Sinai, finding direction and security in the great code of regulations and symbols of forgiveness and salvation offered there.

Some servants seem to prefer the "dark speech." It leaves them with a greater sense of mystery and awe. And it seems to give some religious leaders special influence and power. They are venerated by less knowledgeable servants as "stewards of the mysteries" of God.[5]

But God's "mysteries" are not to be enshrouded in secrecy, like the carefully concealed knowledge of the popular "mystery religions" of Paul's day. God's secrets are to be fully revealed and made known.[6] In fact, the New Testament describes God's most important secret as "Christ himself."[7] And Jesus did not come to hide the truth. On the contrary, he came to make it plain and clear.

Some even look back wistfully at the thunder and lightning of Sinai. "How good it would be," I've heard some say, "if God would raise his voice to our wicked world today!"

Friends like to remember that the cave where God spoke to Elijah in the "still, small voice" was also there at Mount Sinai.[8]

From Servants to Friends

I know many who have welcomed the offer of John 15:15. They enjoy the freedom of friendship so much that they often talk about how they can share this with others. Of course, friendship cannot be pressed on anyone. As God's friend Paul advised, "Let all be fully convinced in their own minds."[9]

All that friends can do is encourage others to look at the same evidence they have found so convincing. And that means all the evidence — including those "more ferocious aspects of the Scriptures." Too often pictures of God and salvation are based on a selection of Biblical passages, rather than on the Bible as a whole. "Here a little, and there a little," some faithful servants say. But what about the rest?

Leftover Parts

It would seem to make good sense that anyone who claims to accept the Bible as trustworthy should build his understanding, his model, his philosophy, his picture of God and salvation on the contents of all sixty-six books. If something in the Bible doesn't seem to fit my model, either I'm misunderstanding the passage, or my model needs enlargement or repair.

When I was 16, I enrolled in an auto mechanics class offered by the high-school I was attending in California. Members of the class became very fond of our highly-respected teacher, Mr. Grubb. He divided us into pairs, and each pair was assigned to a venerable automobile. Our job was to dismantle the moving parts of our car, and especially, of course, the engine. We were to scrape the bearings, grind the valves, and perform certain other services in the way they used to be done 55 years ago.

After that, we were to reassemble all the parts. Then came the acid test. If the car could be started, we would receive a grade. Otherwise . . . Actually I can't remember what the alternative was, for our car started with a bang and a roar. Several students climbed aboard, and we drove it triumphantly around the block.

"What shall we do with the leftover parts?"

174

There was only one problem. We seemed to have several parts left over. Mercifully Mr. Grubb was very kind, and we received our grade anyway. But I certainly wouldn't want to drive that car for any distance. Not without those leftover parts!

Some time ago, I received a printed guide to the study of the Gospel of John. One of the stated purposes of the publication was to encourage people to read the Bible as a whole. I looked with special interest to see what the guide would say about John 16:26. You recall that's the verse where Jesus told his disciples "plainly and clearly" that there would be no need for him to pray the Father for us, for the Father loves us himself.

But there was no comment on that John 16 passage. No comment on its omission, either. When respectful inquiry was made, the author explained that he couldn't find a way to fit that verse into the traditional model. It made me think of my high-school car and all those leftover parts.

The Picture of God in All Sixty-six Books

During the years I have had the privilege of leading groups through all sixty-six books of the Bible, our only concern has been the picture of God. We haven't spent time wondering how he got the dinosaurs into the ark! But we *have* asked what kind of a God would drown all those people.

I remember the day when an 84 year old saint rose to her feet in front of 300 people. "I just want to tell you," she said in a remarkably firm voice, "that I have loved the Lord all of my life. But now that we've gone through all sixty-six books, I not only love him — I *like* him!"

It has been especially enjoyable to go through the Bible with children. They are so candid in their questions and observations.

One afternoon we had just come to the Old Testament teaching about "an eye for an eye and a tooth for a tooth."[10] Questions arose about Jesus having said that we shouldn't do that anymore. Instead, we should turn the other cheek.

I asked the children what they would do if someone knocked out one of their teeth. After several suggestions, eight year old Casey, who sat right beside me, his feet not yet reaching the floor, rendered his carefully thought-out decision.

"First I'd knock out *his* tooth. Then I'd turn the other cheek!"

On another occasion, we were talking about the many references in the Bible to God's destruction of the wicked. I asked the children if their mothers ever said, "You do what I say, or I'll kill you"?

"Yes!" the whole group gleefully responded.

"Do you think they really mean it?" I inquired.

"No, of course not," replied young Tina. "We know it's just a figure of speech."

"Do you think God is just using a figure of speech?" I continued the question. They indicated that they didn't think so. "Then does that mean your mothers love you more than God does?"

Finally Casey was the only one to break the silence. After he had considered the serious implications, all he could say was, "Wow!"

I could have told the children that the best solution to such problems is to stop asking questions and just have faith in God. Of course, that would have been the end of their trip through the Bible. Intelligent children soon tire of simply being told by knowledgeable adults what they ought to believe.

But I'm sure God must love listening to children talk

about him the way our group of youngsters did. And it was the freedom — and safety — to talk candidly about God that kept them reading on book by book through the sixty-six.

"Thank You for All Sixty-six"

On a recent trip to Britain, I heard about a little girl named Leilani, who had written some letters to God. I also learned that, young as she was, she had read through all the books of the Bible. She had decided that the God of all sixty-six books must be a very special Person.

We drove up to Scotland to see her. As we stood together in the back garden of her home in Edinburgh, Leilani read some of her letters.

This one, she said, was her favorite.

Dear God,

Thank you for making me,
and for sixty-six books —
39 in the Old Testament,
*   27 in the New —*
so we can find out about you.

            Your friend,
            Leilani.

"I see there's a P. S. at the end," I observed.
"Oh, just a little one. It says, 'We all know it's true.'"

"That means," she explained, "that we know that what the Bible says is true."

I know you would love Leilani. And Leilani is one of God's friends.

p in northwest En-
gland, close to the
border of Scotland, there lives a strong but gentle shepherd. We
heard that recently he had become a Christian. So we went to
find out what had led him to make this decision.

With the help of a well-trained dog, he led his flock down
the hill in our direction. Then we watched the birth of triplets
and marvelled at how skillfully he handled both the mother and
the three new lambs. As he stood there, holding one of the
thousand baby lambs he helped deliver every year, I had a chance
to ask him how he had made up his mind to become a believer.

"It was me friend Alice," he said, nodding toward a woman
with a wonderfully friendly face.

"Tell us what she did," I requested.

"Oh, she just took me through the Bible, and it seemed to
come out right."

We learned more about Alice. She had gone through all
sixty-six books and loved the picture of God she had found. She
was very active in her little country church, and even preached
from time to time when the pastor was away. Not long ago she
sent me a recording of her sermon on the Good Shepherd. My

*"She took me
through the
Bible, and it
seemed to come
out right."*

wife pronounced it the best sermon she had ever heard on the subject.

One of the marks of true friendship with God is jealousy for our heavenly Friend's reputation. Abraham, Moses and Job all demonstrated such loyalty. So did Alice. She wanted God to be seen as he really is, and it won the heart of the shepherd.

I notice that friends of God are especially concerned that their children see God as a Friend. After visiting so many empty churches in Britain, we attended one in London that was said to be overflowing with worshippers every week. Four vivacious young girls let me talk with them after the service.

"When you get to heaven, who would you rather meet first — God the Father, or Jesus the Son?"

Without a moment's hesitation, one of the girls replied, "It wouldn't make any difference. Jesus said, 'If you've seen me, you've seen the Father.'" I wondered if some friend of God had helped that bright young girl.

When I ask what should be done to bring disillusioned people back to church, some say that such doubters should be told to stop asking so many questions and show a little more faith. Some even add that warning from Hebrews that "No one can please God without faith."[1] To me, this is the way servants talk. And this approach is just what has turned so many people in the world against God.

Friends of God would want to understand why people like Lorraine and her family feel that Christian teachings have no meaning any more. There has indeed been a great deal of "dark speech" in talking about God and salvation.

If Jesus were here in person, he would go and talk plainly and clearly to Lorraine and her gentle family, to Barry the butcher, to the gravedigger and the motorbikers. As God's children, they deserve an opportunity to understand.

It is the high privilege of God's friends to serve as his "mediators" to such people, as Moses did to the Children of Israel.

When I asked a young Christian schoolboy what he thought should be done for people like Lorraine, he replied quickly, "Just tell them stories about Jesus."

To tell about Jesus is to tell about the upper room and what the Lord said and did to his disciples there. It means to explain that God values nothing higher than the freedom and friendship of his children everywhere.

The Father is just like Jesus."

To tell about Jesus means inviting people to ask *more* questions, not less. Not just quibbling questions, of course, but questions aimed at understanding the truth.

Those who venture to speak for God should be the first to encourage such inquiry. To follow Christ's example means to set people free to say respectfully to the most erudite preacher, "I don't understand what you just said about God. Forgive me for having to say this, but to me it was all just 'dark speech.' "

To follow Christ's example also means to be very respectful of servants. If in their fear of God they need the assurance that they have a Friend between, friends of God will tell them that indeed they have such a friendly Intercessor. Perhaps later there will come a chance to explain that the Friend between is God.

To servants, the greatest compliment they could hear from God is, "Well done, you good and faithful servant."

How could anyone ask for anything more?

To those who have accepted the offer of John 15:15, there is an even greater compliment in store: "Thank you, my children, for telling the truth. Thank you for being my friends."

Another LOOK

I believe that the most important of all Christian beliefs is the one that brings joy and assurance to God's friends everwhere—the truth about our heavenly Father that was confirmed at such cost by the life and death of his Son.

God is not the kind of person his enemies have made him out to be—arbitrary, unforgiving and severe. God is just as loving and trustworthy as his Son, just as willing to forgive and heal. Though infinite in majesty and power, our Creator is an equally gracious Person who values nothing higher than the freedom, dignity, and individuality of his intelligent creatures—that

at GOD

their love, their faith, their willingness to listen and obey, may be freely given. He even prefers to regard us not as servants but as friends. This is the truth revealed through all the books of Scripture. This is the everlasting Good News that wins the trust and admiration of God's loyal children throughout the universe.

Like Abraham and Moses—the ones God spoke of as his trusted friends—God's friends today want to speak well and truly of our heavenly Father. They covet as the highest of all commendations the words of God about Job: "He has said of me what is right."

EPILOGUE

his book began with the offer of friendship made by the Sovereign of the universe.

It is the King himself who says to his servants, "I'd rather you be my friends."

CHAPTER NOTES

Prologue

1. The "Sixty-six" include the 39 books of the Old Testament which are recognized by most Christians and Jews, and the 27 books of the New Testament accepted by most Christians.

Chapter 1

1. The Scottish word for "church."
2. In England, these are the familiar terms for mothers and grandmothers.
3. In England, decent means well-behaved, respectable, and kind.

Chapter 2

1. An upstairs room where Jesus ate the Passover supper with his disciples. *See* Luke 22:12,13.
2. An old English term for letter.
3. *See* Revelation 7:11,12.
4. *See* John 12:44,45; 14:9; 15:15.
5. *See* John 16:27.
6. Isaiah 9:6, KJV.
7. Jim Jones was the leader of a religious cult that committed mass suicide in 1978 in the jungles of Guyana.
8. *See* Daniel 3.
9. *See* Genesis 18.
10. *See* Genesis 18:25.
11. *See* Exodus 32:7–14; Numbers 14:11–19.
12. *See* Exodus 33:11; Numbers 12:8.
13. *See* Job 29:1–4; 30:20, GNB.
14. *See* Job 16:2.
15. *See* Job 37:20, GNB.
16. *See* Job 23:3–7, GNB.
17. *See* Job 42:7,8, GNB.
18. *See* Exodus 20.
19. *See* Galatians 3:19.
20. Zechariah 3:4.

21. John 15:12,17, REB.
22. John 15:14.
23. The sad story is told in 2 Samuel 15–18.

Chapter 3

1. *See* John 14:8.
2. *See* Genesis 6–8.
3. *See* Genesis 18:16–19:29.
4. *See* Leviticus 10:1–11.
5. *See* Numbers 16.
6. *See* Joshua 7.
7. *See* 1 Kings 18.
8. 1 Corinthians 10:4, NEB.
9. *See* Exodus 19:10–25.
10. Exodus 20:18,19, GNB.
11. Exodus 33:11, NRSV.
12. *See* Numbers 14:11–19.
13. *See* 1 Kings 19:12.
14. *See* Luke 19:41–44; 13:34; Matthew 23:37.
15. Proverbs 9:10, GNB.
16. *See* Hebrews 12:6.
17. Proverbs 3:11,12, NRSV.
18. Hebrews 12:7–11, REB.
19. *See* 1 Kings 19:9–13.
20. Proverbs 18:24, NRSV.
21. Acts 8:1, NRSV.
22. Acts 7:60, REB.
23. Luke 23:34, NRSV.
24. Acts 9:1, NRSV.
25. Aramaic. See Acts 26:14.
26. *See* Romans 1:1.
27. *See* Acts 22:10.
28. Acts 22:13, REB.
29. A word used for assistants to physicians, kings, the Sanhedrin, or in a synagogue. Some versions offer the translation "minister," as also in Luke 1:2, "ministers of the word."

30. Acts 22:14,15, REB.
31. *See* 1 Corinthians 11:1.
32. *See* Romans 14:5.
33. *See* Romans 14:1–23.
34. 2 Corinthians 10:10, NRSV.
35. The whole story is told in 2 Corinthians.
36. *See* Joshua 7:1–29.
37. *See* Joshua 1:18.
38. *See* Matthew 10:29,30 and Luke 12:6,7.

Chapter 4

1. *See* Daniel 3.
2. Daniel 3:6 REB.
3. Daniel 3:14,15, REB.
4. Daniel 2:47, REB.
5. *See* Exodus 3.
6. Daniel 3:24,25, REB.
7. Daniel 3:28, REB.
8. *See* Romans 14:5.
9. Daniel 3:29, REB.
10. Daniel 4:27, NIV.
11. *See* Psalm 135:6.
12. Daniel 4:32,35,37,2,3, REB.
13. *See* Matthew 19:26.
14. Zechariah 4:6, NIV.
15. Zechariah 8:3, NIV and REB.
16. Zechariah 8:4,5, NIV.
17. Zechariah 8:22,23, niv.
18. *See* Revelation 12:7–9.
19. *See* James 2:19.
20. *See* 1 Kings 11:7,8 and 2 Kings 23:10.
21. *See* Romans 1:17.
22. *See* John 13:1–20.

Chapter 5

1. *See* Acts 16:25–34.
2. *See* James 2:19.

3. Hebrews 1:1,2; John 14:9.
4. See Revelation 12:7–9.
5. *See* John 8:44.
6. *See* Genesis 3.
7. *See* John 1:1–3; Colossians 1:16.
8. *See* Matthew 24:23,24.
9. Matthew 24:4,5, GNB.
10. 1 John 4:1, GNB.
11. *See* Revelation 13:8,12–14, GNB.
12. Deuteronomy 13:1–3, GNB.
13. 1 Kings 13:8,9, GNB.
14. 1 Kings 13:18, GNB.
15. 1 Thessalonians 5:21, NIV.
16. Luke 24:21, GNB.
17. 2 Corinthians 11:14, REB, NIV.

Chapter 6

1. *See* Exodus 32.
2. Matthew 7:6, NRSV.
3. Numbers 12:3, NRSV.
4. *See* Isaiah 53:3,7.
5. *See* Deuteronomy 18:15–18.
6. *See* Luke 24:27,44; *see also* Acts 3:17–26.
7. *See* Luke 9:28-36; *see also* Matthew 17:1–8, Mark 9:2–8.
8. Numbers 12:6–8, NRSV.
9. Exodus 33:11, NRSV.
10. John 16:25, NRSV.
11. John 16:29, NRSV.
12. John 16:32, NRSV.
13. John 16:25–28, NIV.
14. *See* Leviticus 16.
15. Exodus 32:11–14, NRSV.
16. *See* 1 John 2:1; Romans 8:34.
17. *See* John 17:6–26.
18. *See* Matthew 5:17.
19. *See* Exodus 20:18,19.
20. *See* Isaiah 9:6.

Chapter 7

1. *See* Matthew 18:1; Mark 9:34; Luke 9:46–48.
2. *See* Luke 22:24.
3. *See* Mark 10:35-45; Matthew 20:20–28.
4. Galatians 3:19, NRSV.
5. Galatians 3:19, NRSV.
6. 1 Timothy 1:9,10, GNB.
7. *See* Acts 17:22–31.
8. *See* 1 Corinthians 2:1–5.
9. 2 Peter 3:16, REB.
10. Galatians 5:22, NRSV.
11. Galatians 3:24,25.
12. Isaiah 29:13, NRSV.
13. Mark 2:6, KJV.
14. Jeremiah 31:33, NRSV.
15. Romans 7:22, NRSV.
16. Hosea 6:6, Phillips.
17. Jeremiah 31:34, NRSV.
18. 1 Corinthians 8:3, NRSV.
19. *See* James 2:8–12, NRSV.
20. Romans 13:8–10, REB; *see also* Matthew 22:36–40; Deuteronomy 6:5; Leviticus 19:18.
21. 1 Corinthians 13:4–6, NRSV.
22. *See* Genesis 22:8; Hebrews 11:19.

Chapter 8

1. James 4:17, KJV.
2. Romans 3:31, NRSV.
3. *See* Romans 2:15.
4. Romans 14:23.
5. Ephesians 4:14, NRSV.
6. James 1:6–8, GNB.
7. Hebrews 5:13, 14, NRSV.
8. Numbers 20:8–12, NIV.
9. Deuteronomy 3:23–26, NIV.
10. Deuteronomy 32:51, NIV.
11. *See* Romans 2:4; 10:17.

12. *See* Deuteronomy 34:1–6.
13. *See* Matthew 17:3; Mark 9:4; Luke 9:30.
14. "God said it! I believe it! That settles it!"
15. Latin, "justitia."
16. Mesopotamia is mentioned several times, such as Genesis 24:10 and Acts 7:2.
17. Hebrews 9:22, KJV.

Chapter 9

1. One of the small cities that was destroyed with Sodom and Gomorrah. (*See* Genesis 10:19; 14:2,8; Deuteronomy 29:23)
2. *See* previous note.
3. Hosea 11:1–8, GNB.
4. Romans 1:18–28, NRSV, emphasis supplied.
5. Matthew 19:14, NRSV.
6. *See* Luke 9:51–55; 19:10.
7. *See* Luke 8:49–56.
8. Luke 23:34, GNB. Your version may not include these words of Jesus, because some of the ancient manuscripts omit them. See the whole story in Matthew 27, Mark 15, Luke 23, and John 19.
9. *See* Matthew 27:46.
10. 2 Corinthians 5:21, NRSV.
11. Romans 3:25,26, my own translation.
12. Mark 14:34, NIV.
13. Luke 22:43,44, NIV. If your version does not include Luke's report, it is because it is not included in some manuscripts.
14. *See* 1 Timothy 3:16; 1 Peter 1:12.
15. *See* John 16:26,27.
16. John 10:18, NRSV.
17. *See* Romans 6:23.
18. *See* John 5:39,40.
19. *See* John 8.
20. Matthew 25:41, NRSV.
21. Isaiah 33:14,15, NRSV.
22. Exodus 24:17, NRSV.
23. Daniel 7:9,10, NRSV.

24. *See* Ezekiel 1:28, NRSV.
25. Ezekiel 28:14, NRSV.
26. Exodus 33:20.
27. *See* Exodus 34:29–35.
28. Hebrews 1:3, Phillips.
29. Philippians 2:7,NRSV.
30. *See* Genesis 3:8–10.
31. 2 Peter 3:9, NIV.

Chapter 10

1. *See* Hebrews 12:21, NRSV.
2. John 8:2–11, NIV.
3. Luke 7:37, REB.
4. Luke 7:39,40, NIV.
5. *See* John 5:1–15.
6. Luke 22:24, NRSV.
7. *See* Luke 22:54–62.
8. *See* Matthew 27:3–5.
9. *See* Luke 8:2.
10. *See* John 20:17.
11. *See* Mark 16:7; *see also* John 20:19.
12. Isaiah 38:17, NRSV.
13. Micah 7:19, GNB.
14. 1 Kings 3:14, NRSV.
15. Acts 13:22, NIV. Compare 1 Samuel 13:14.
16. *See* Romans 1:29.

Chapter 11

1 *See* Romans 5:1.
2. *See* Romans 7:19,24.
3. Romans 7:18–24, NIV.
4. Romans 7:25, NIV.
5. Philippians 3:5,6, REB.
6. *See* Leviticus 19:17.
7. Some Christians divide the Commandment about not coveting into 9 and 10.

8. *See* Romans 8:1.
9. Romans 8:3, NRSV.
10. Romans 8:3, GNB.

Chapter 12

1. Romans 5:10,11, GNB.
2. John 17:20,21, NRSV.
3. John 17:22, NRSV.
4. *See* Matthew 20:28.
5. John 12:32,33, GNB.
6. Ephesians 1:10, REB.
7. Colossians 1:20, NRSV.
8. *See* 1 John 3:4.
9. *See* Romans 14:23.
10. Ephesians 4:13, REB.
11. 2 Corinthians 5:17–20, GNB.
12. Luke 15:20–24, REB.
13. Luke 15:29–32, GNB.

Chapter 13

1. Deuteronomy 1:6,7, NIV.
2. Judges 21:25, GNB; *see also* Judges 17:6.
3. *See* Exodus 3:8.
4. *See* Isaiah 58:13.
5. *See* 1 Corinthians 4:1.
6. *See* Colossians 1:25,26.
7. *See* Colossians 2:2,3.
8. *See* 1 Kings 19:8–13.
9. Romans 14:5, NRSV.
10. Exodus 21:24; Leviticus 24:20; Deuteronomy 19:21; Matthew 5:38–42.

Chapter 14

1. Hebrews 11:6, GNB.

THE ARTIST

Susan Kelley completed a Bachelor of Science degree in psychology from Northern Arizona University, with a minor in art. Her fascination with art brought her to California State University, Long Beach, where she received her Master of Arts degree in drawing and painting in 1981.

Susan's graduate and postgraduate studies included work in portraiture, illustration, and graphic design with sojourns in Europe for independent study in larger galleries and museums.

In addition to private portrait commissions for an international clientele, Susan has done illustrations for such clients as *Reader's Digest*, McDonald Charities, Los Angeles Children's Hospital, NBC Television, California State University, Galoob Toys, Maranatha! Music, National Medical Home Care, Memorial Hospital Long Beach, and Wherehouse Records.

Susan is a versatile artist, known for her colors and painterly style, and her sensitive renditions of people. Her original art has been on display in Los Angeles exhibitions at the Museum of Science and Industry; Foote, Cone and Belding; the Fashion Institute; and California State University.

Susan lives in California with her husband, Kevin Harkey — a successful cartoonist — their son, Hollis, and, daughter Shannon.

THE MODELS

More than forty wonderful friends volunteered their time to model for the pictures in this book. In case you should happen to meet one of these friends, I really owe them a word or two of explanation:

The top-hatted traveling salesman is a church leader in Britain and has a Ph.D. from St. Andrews University in Scotland.

The king is a seminary professor in Russia and Czechoslovakia, who truly exemplifies what it means to be a serving friend.

Saul on the Damascus road is an anesthesiologist, who would be happy to meet Christ on any road.

The false prophet is a trusted dentist, who would never think of misleading anyone.

The worried patient already knows what will happen to those who refuse their medicine. So does her surgeon husband, who modeled Moses.

The forgiving Jesus on the cross is a highly-respected attorney.

No one took his modeling more seriously than Brad, the boy admiring his older brother.

Other models included a radiologist, a school counselor, a teacher, and a doctor of preventive medicine. And many were students — from first grade through medical school — including three of my grandchildren.

Four pictures were painted from our video documentary about Christianity in Britain, *One of the Lads*.

Incidentally, the butler is the author — trying to look like a faithful servant.

THE AUTHOR

Graham Maxwell was emeritus professor of New Testament at Loma Linda University. He was born in England, attended college in California, and earned his Ph.D. in Biblical studies, New Testament, from the University of Chicago Divinity School.

His dissertation dealt with the elements of interpretation that have entered into the translation of the New Testament, and especially Romans. Romans continued to be a subject of his research and writing for many years. Other publications include *I Want to Be Free, You Can Trust the Bible, Can God Be Trusted?* And *Be Careful Who You Trust!*

For nineteen years he taught Bible and Biblical languages to college and ministerial students at Pacific Union College. In 1961 he moved to Loma Linda to serve as director of the division of religion and teach Bible to medical, dental, and other professional students.

His favorite course was a year-long trip through the whole Bible to discover the picture of God in each of the sixty-six books. He taught this course over 135 times, not only in the classroom, but in churches and homes, to groups ranging in size from a dozen to 700.

People in 118 different countries have shared in this book by book study of the Bible with the help of recordings. But as one man wrote from the Falkland Islands, "I want you to know that I always read the book in the Bible before I listen to those recordings."

Maxwell watched the effect of such Bible study on over 10,000 people. "Something seems to happen," he said, "when people of all cultures discover in the Bible a consistent picture of God—an infinitely powerful but equally gracious Person, who values nothing higher than their freedom and friendship." That's what led to the writing of this book.

Maxwell taught a weekly Bible class for 250 members for nearly 50 years that was recorded and sent to over 1,000 addresses around the world.

Graham and Rosalyn, the girl he met in college, were married for 67 years. They had three daughters, 7 grandchildren, and 10 great-grandchildren.

SERVANTS OR FRIENDS?
Another Look at God

DESIGN
By Elliot Hutkin, Susan Kelley, and Linda Wheeler

TYPOGRAPHY
by Linda Wheeler
Win Graphics Prepress
in Kennerley and University

PRINTING
in 2-color on acid-free ∞ Somerset Matte
Hardcover, dust jacket, and softcover printed in 4-color

BINDING
Smyth-sewn

PRODUCTION
Printed and bound by the Production Staff of
LSC Communications, Crawfordsville, Indiana
Special thanks to Perry Martin Team